THE
Couple's
Kitchen

A NEWLYWEDS cookbook

THE
Couple's
Kitchen

A NEWLYWEDS cookbook

RYLAND PETERS & SMALL
LONDON • NEW YORK

Designer Maria Lee-Warren
Editors Gillian Haslam and Miriam Catley
Production Controller Silvia La Greca
Art Director Leslie Harrington
Editorial Director Julia Charles

Indexer Hilary Bird

First published in 2014
by Ryland Peters & Small
20–21 Jockey's Fields
London WC1R 4BW
and
519 Broadway, 5th Floor
New York NY 10012

www.rylandpeters.com

Design and photographs © Ryland Peters & Small 2014

ISBN: 978-1-84975-499-6

10 9 8 7 6 5 4 3 2 1

A CIP record for this book is available from the British Library.

US Library of Congress Cataloging-in-Publication data has been applied for.

Printed and bound in China

Contents

Getting Started

One of the pleasures of settling into married life is enjoying time together preparing good food for yourselves and for loved ones. From long, leisurely brunches and intimate dinners for two to spontaneous kitchen suppers and lively family entertaining you will find all the inspiration you need to prepare delicious meals at home in this book.

Breakfast & Brunch provides relaxed recipes to start your day, such as Blueberry Pancakes and Eggs Benedict. Soups & Small Bites are perfect for light lunches or appetizers – try a Smoky Chorizo and Bean Soup, Blinis with Smoked Salmon and Crème Fraîche, or Pancetta and Fennel Puffs. There's a go-to selection of Salads & Sides with an elegant Salad of Truffled French Beans and classic Roasted Vegetables and Roast Potatoes perfect for pairing with any hearty dish. In Just the Two of Us you'll find meals to enjoy together, many of which are speedy to make and perfect for weeknights, such as Simple Basil and Tomato Risotto. Or why not take turns to choose something more impressive for 'date night', such as Halibut with Fennel, Olives and Tomato?

Spending your weekends with family and friends? Feeding a Crowd offers the solution, with delicious dishes such as Glorious Golden Fish Pie or Traditional Texas Chilli. Desserts and Cheese Plates offers ideas to satisfy a sweet tooth or those who prefer a savoury end to a meal. Choose from decadent Chilled Lemon Soufflés perfect for summer entertaining, or share a slice of indulgent Rocky Road Cheesecake. More delicious treats are to be found in Baking Days. Enjoy homemade breads, as well as sweet bakes, from simple slices and cupcakes to larger cakes for birthdays. Holiday Celebrations bring their own culinary challenges so here you'll find essential recipes for hosting the perfect Thanksgiving dinner or Christmas Day feast with all the trimmings. In Drinks there is an irresistible selection of cocktails and punches, perfect for relaxed entertaining or catering for large parties during the holiday season. Finally, themed Menu Planners group recipes together, enabling you to create exciting meals for every occasion.

Pantry & Storecupboard

*A well-stocked pantry will enable you to whip up a delicious meal at a moment's notice —
from a simple pasta dish to a hearty risotto. Investing in some storecupboard essentials
will also help to keep your food budget to a minimum. For special occasions, dip in to the
list of luxurious items for ingredients that will really lift your menu to new heights.*

Staples
2–3 packages pasta, various
    shapes
2–3 packages rice – basmati, Thai
    fragrant, long grain, risotto
baking powder
brown sugar, white/granulated
    sugar, caster/superfine sugar
cans of chopped tomatoes,
    kidney beans, chickpeas,
    anchovies in oil
coconut cream or milk
coffee and tea
cornflour/cornstarch
dried lentils
egg or rice noodles
plain/all-purpose, self-raising/
    rising flour, wholemeal/
    wholewheat flour, gram flour

Oils and vinegars
balsamic vinegar
extra virgin olive oil
olive oil
red and white wine vinegar
sunflower or peanut oil

Seasonings & flavourings
black peppercorns
coarse sea salt
honey
mustard
soy sauce (light and dark)
Worcestershire sauce

Spices
crushed dried red chillies
ground cinnamon and
    cinnamon sticks
ground coriander
ground cumin
ground turmeric
sweet paprika
whole nutmeg

Fresh produce
(bell) peppers
carrots
celery
garlic
ginger
herbs
lemons, limes, oranges
apples and pears
onions (red and white)
potatoes
fresh red and green chillies
tomatoes
salad leaves
cucumber

Refrigerator
Cheddar, Parmesan
cream cheese
eggs
milk
plain yogurt
unsalted butter

In the freezer
mixed red berries
frozen peas
ice cubes
pastry
vanilla ice cream

Extra items
Staples
unsweetened cocoa powder
bread (strong) flour
couscous, cracked wheat,
    quinoa, polenta, rolled oats
ground almonds, flaked almonds,
    pine nuts
raisins and sultanas
glacé/candied cherries

Oils and vinegars
sesame oil or walnut oil

Seasonings & flavourings
brandy
capers
horseradish sauce
Marsala or sherry
olives
red wine
sun-dried tomatoes and peppers
Thai fish sauce
tamari
tomato purée/paste
vanilla beans/pods

Luxuries
dark/bittersweet chocolate
dried porcini mushrooms
goji berries
orange flower water
saffron threads
truffle oil

Cooking Essentials

Gradually filling your cupboards with cooking equipment and utensils that you will use to prepare meals for many years to come is a fun part of homemaking. If you love to bake then adding to your bakeware arsenal will enable you to whip up simple muffins or homebaked breads in a snap.

Breakfast and brunch

Blender

Coffeemaker, cafetière, espresso machine and/or coffee grinder

Juicer

Kettle

Toaster

In your cupboard

Casserole

Colander

Small frying pan

Large frying pan

Griddle

Grill pan

Non-reactive pan

Roasting pans

Saucepans

Sieve/strainer

Steamer

Wok

Baking

Baking sheets

Baking stone

Bread scraper

Cupcake/muffin pans

Electric mixer

Food processor

Hand mixer

Kitchen scales

Measuring cups and spoons

Ramekins

Rolling pin

Round and square cake pans

Set of mixing bowls

Springform pan

Souffle dish

Wire cooling rack

Utensils

Basting brush

Can opener

Corkscrew

Kitchen scissors

Knife sharpener

Ladle

Large metal spoon

Large slotted metal spoon

Lemon juicer

Metal whisk

Olive oil drizzler

Potato masher

Salad servers

Set of sharp knives

Metal skewers

Rubber spatula

Tongs

Vegetable peeler

Wooden spoons

Box grater

Carving board

Chopping board

Mortar and pestle

Pizza stone

Salad spinner

Salt and pepper mills

Thermometer

Dishtowels

Oven mitts

Cooking timer

Dining Essentials

It wasn't that long ago that owning a smart dinner service was essential. Today entertaining is a much more informal affair, and keeping fine china 'just for best' seems a wasteful concept. Now that we are far more likely to have friends round for a relaxed kitchen supper than to serve a formal dinner in the dining room, we need dinnerware we can use whatever the occasion.

If you are starting a collection from scratch, you don't need to spend a lot of money. Choose a good basic set that you can use every day and then dress up for parties; a simple design or a plain colour will give you most flexibility when it comes to dressing the table. Invest in as many settings as you require (a standard service for eight is a good starting point) and think about which pieces you really need. Individual cereal, soup and dessert bowls, or one dish that does it all? Will you get more use from capacious pasta plates or streamlined dinner plates? If a matching set is a priority, check that your chosen china is a stock item so that broken pieces will be easily replaceable.

Today, there are so many styles of tableware available, from rustic earthenware to colourful melamine to delicate vintage china, and most of us end up with a combination of these different types. Try to match the crockery to the occasion and to the food you are serving; delicate desserts, for example, call for dainty plates. The advantage of simple white china is that is goes with everything, but patterned services or even a completely mismatched collection can work well, too.

If you need to add to your crockery cupboard, you'll be spoilt for choice. Homeware stores on the high street and the internet sport a vast array of modern designs; junk stores and auction houses can both be good sources of inexpensive vintage pieces. What you end up with will depend largely on your taste and your budget, of course, but don't forget to consider the practicalities, too. Do you have enough storage space for that stack of bamboo bowls and will you mind hand-washing those pretty retro plates?

Households used to own a vast array of different pieces but most modern canteens will contain the bare minimum: a set of knives, forks, dessert- and teaspoons is standard. A simple collection should be enough for everyday, but it can be useful to add some extras over time. Steak knives, for example, are not part of a basic canteen but can be handy if you eat a lot of red meat; ditto fish knives, if you are a fan of seafood. Dessert forks are rarely supplied and are perfect for tea parties but a set of dainty cake forks can often be bought separately.

China
8 dinner plates
8 side plates
8 soup bowls
8 dessert plates or dishes
8 cups and saucers

Serving dishes
2 platters
Serving bowls
Sauce or gravy boat
Water jug/pitcher
Creamer/cream jug
Sugar bowl
Teapot and/or coffee pot
small dishes, variety of

Glassware
8 water glasses
8 red wine glasses
8 white wine glasses
8 juice glasses
8 highball glasses
8 champagne flutes
8 brandy glasses
8 martini glasses
8 margarita glasses
8 liqueur glasses

Cutlery
8 dinner forks
8 salad forks
8 dinner knives
8 butter knives
8 steak knives
8 soup spoons

8 dessert spoons and
   forks
8 teaspoons

Serving pieces
2 ladles – 1 large and
   1 small
Sugar spoons
Salad servers
1 large, three-pronged
   fork
2–3 serving spoons
Pie server

Table Linen
Tablecloth
8 napkins
Heatproof mats

Kitchen Wisdom

From rescuing a lumpy sauce to knowing just how much wine to serve at a dinner party the following hints and tips will help you prepare and serve your meals with confidence.

Cooking

Fruit

If you need the juice and the zest from a citrus fruit, remove the zest first (you can freeze it in an ice-cube tray for future use) before squeezing the juice.

To peel peaches or plums, plunge them into a bowl of boiling water for 1 minute, then remove and plunge into cold or iced water to stop the cooking process. When cool enough to handle, the skins will peel off easily.

Rinse fresh berries such as raspberries and strawberries just before serving, as they will deteriorate quickly once washed.

Onions

To minimize tears when preparing an onion, try peeling it under cold running water and leaving the root end intact when chopping.

Chilli/chile safety tip

The natural oils in fresh chillies may cause irritation to your skin and eyes. When preparing them, wear disposable gloves or pull a small plastic bag over each hand, secured with an elastic band around the wrist, to create a glove.

Stock

To remove fat from the surface of stock, pour the stock into a jug/pitcher and add a few ice cubes. When the fat has set around the ice, lift it off and discard.

Sauce rescue remedy

To rescue a lumpy sauce or gravy, whisk it vigorously, using a balloon whisk, until smooth. Alternatively, pour the lumpy sauce into a small blender or food processor and blend for about 1 minute, until smooth. You can also pour the sauce or gravy through a fine sieve/strainer into a clean pan.

Marinades

An easy way to marinate meat or poultry is to use a plastic food bag. Put the meat in the bag, add the marinade, and seal. Shake the bag, ensuring the meat is completely covered in the marinade. Once the meat is marinated, remove the meat and discard the bag. Never save and reuse marinades.

Wine

Freeze leftover wine in an ice-cube tray. Once solid, transfer the wine cubes to a freezer bag. The wine cubes can be added to casseroles, stews and gravies for extra flavour.

Baking

Butter

Instead of rubbing butter into flour using your fingertips, try coarsely grating chilled butter into the flour, then using a pastry blender or fork to work it in. This keeps the mixture as cool as possible. A food processor will also do the job quickly and easily.

If you are creaming butter for a cake mixture and it is slightly too cool, wrap a warm, damp kitchen towel around the bowl and continue to cream.

Milk

To help prevent milk from scorching during cooking, heat it gently in a heavy-based saucepan or double-boiler. Rinsing the pan in cold water before adding the milk may also keep it from boiling over.

Bread

When making bread, make sure the liquid is very warm (115–120°F) but not hot. If it is too hot it will kill the yeast. If it is too cold, it will inhibit the yeast's action.

Measure ingredients accurately. Too much flour will result in a dry and crumbly loaf; too much liquid may give a dense, flat loaf. If too much yeast is used, the bread is likely to stale very quickly.

Don't be tempted to add too much flour to the work surface when kneading, as this may make the dough tough and dry. A light sprinkling of flour should suffice.

Cakes

Toss dried fruit, glacé/candied cherries and nuts in a little flour or ground almonds before adding them to a cake batter. This should prevent the fruit or nuts from sinking to the bottom of the cake and keep them evenly dispersed during baking. If you wash the fruit, dry it well before using.

If you do not have a piping bag, use a strong plastic bag. Snip a corner off the bottom of the bag, insert a nozzle, then fill with icing/frosting and pipe as normal. Discard the bag after use.

When making muffins, buns, or cupcakes, lightly spray the paper cases with vegetable oil before use. They should then peel off more easily after baking.

Pastry

If you don't have a rolling pin, use a straight-sided wine bottle instead. If possible, chill the bottle before rolling to keep the pastry cool as you work

Brushing the base of an unbaked pastry shell with egg white or beaten egg will help prevent it becoming soggy. If you're baking a pastry shell blind, remove the beans and brush the base with egg 5 minutes before the end of the cooking time. An alternative is to brush a cold, baked pastry shell with a thin layer of melted chocolate. Let the chocolate set before adding the cold filling.

Cookies

An easy way to transfer sticky cookie dough to a baking sheet is to use a small ice cream scoop. Dip the scoop into a bowl of cold water between each use to ensure an easy release. This also saves your hands getting messy.

Honey, syrup and jam

When measuring sticky foods such as honey, syrup or molasses, lightly spray the measuring spoon or jug with oil first. The sticky ingredient should slip out of the spoon or jug easily. Alternatively, use a metal measuring spoon dipped in hot water.

Chocolate

If you add a liquid to melted chocolate, warm it first, as cold liquid may cause the melted chocolate to solidify. Alternatively, add a small amount of liquid to solid chocolate pieces, then melt the chocolate and liquid together. If the chocolate seizes, add a little more liquid and gently heat and stir until it becomes smooth again.

Entertaining

Cut two slices in a whole pie or cake before removing any portions. This will make it much easier to remove a neat and intact first slice.

Slice whole fresh strawberries, keeping the slices attached to the green tops, then fan out the slices and use to decorate desserts and salads.

Freeze small pieces of fruit in ice cubes and add them to drinks and cocktails, for extra appeal.

At drinks parties, one 75 cl bottle of wine or champagne will give about 6 glasses. Allow at least 2 glasses per person.

If you need to chill a bottle of white or sparkling wine quickly, put it in the freezer for about 30 minutes, and no longer than 45 minutes. Set a timer, otherwise you may forget and end up with an exploded bottle!

Warm up a bottle of red wine by putting it in an ice bucket full of warm water (at a temperature of about 68°F) for 20–30 minutes.

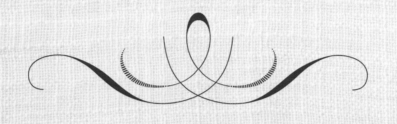

Breakfast & Brunch

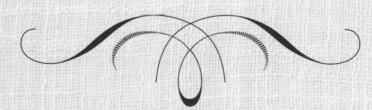

Banana, Honey & Wheatgerm Lassi

Lassi is a cooling Indian drink which can be sweet or savoury. In the summer try adding a handful of ice before blending it for a more chilled drink. If you like ripe bananas, let the skins become speckled for a more intense experience.

2 bananas, peeled

2 teaspoons clear honey

100 g/½ cup plain yogurt

150 ml/⅔ cup whole milk

1 tablespoon wheatgerm or wheat bran

Serves 2

Put the bananas, honey, yogurt and milk in a blender and blend until smooth. Taste and add a little more honey if you think it needs it. Stir in the wheatgerm and blend briefly just to mix. Divide between 2 tall glasses and serve with straws big enough for the wheatgerm not to cause blockages.

Cashew Nut & Mango Smoothie

It's easy to forget how milky blended cashew nuts are, but they do make brilliant dairy-free smoothies. When blended with mango, cashew nuts make a super-thick smoothie verging on dessert territory. You could also use soft berries or bananas.

50 g/⅓ cup shelled cashew nuts, soaked overnight in cold water

1 ripe mango, peeled, pitted and roughly chopped

1 teaspoon linseed

Serves 2

Drain the cashew nuts and put in a blender with 150 ml/⅔ cup water. Blend until you have a smooth, nutty milk. Add the chopped mango. Blend again, then stir in the linseed. Divide between 2 tumblers and serve.

Raspberry, Strawberry & Orange Juice

Keep raspberries in your freezer for a rainy day as they add body to smoothies as well as a sharp burst of fruity flavour. The raspberries will make the drink lovely and icy.

125 g/1 cup frozen raspberries

125 g/1 cup strawberries, hulled

400 ml/1⅔ cups freshly squeezed orange juice

Serves 2–4

Put the raspberries, strawberries and orange juice in a blender and blend until smooth. Divide between 2–4 tumblers and serve.

Bircher Muesli

This muesli has the type of texture you either love or hate. There is something comforting about its soggy sweetness — but if you prefer crunchy try the granola, below. The muesli will keep for 2–3 days in the fridge, but in that case, leave the apple out so it doesn't brown.

125 g/1 cup rolled oats

75 g/½ cup (golden) raisins

175 ml/¾ cup apple juice

juice of 1 lemon

100 g/¼ cup plain yogurt

1 apple, cored, peeled and grated

3 tablespoons flaked/slivered almonds

mixed summer berries, to serve

honey, to serve

Serves 2

Put the oats and raisins in a large dish. Pour over the apple and lemon juices. Cover with a dish cloth and let soak overnight. Alternatively place in an airtight container and refrigerate, especially if it is very hot.

The next morning when you're ready for breakfast, stir the yogurt, apple and almonds into the soaked muesli. Divide between 4–6 bowls, scatter some brightly coloured berries over the top and finish with a zigzag of (clear) honey.

Nutty Honey Granola

Mmmm, crunchy honeyed granola. This version is very sweet and crunchy and quite rich so you don't need a lot. The trick is to get it to brown evenly, so you need it to be spread out and to turn it during roasting. Don't let it become too dark or it gets bitter.

125 g/½ cup maple syrup

125 g/½ cup (clear) honey

4 tablespoons sunflower oil

250 g/2 cups rolled oats

75 g/⅔ cup shelled almonds, roughly chopped

75 g/⅔ cup shelled Brazil nuts, roughly chopped

50 g/⅓ cup pumpkin seeds

½ teaspoon salt

100 g/⅔ cup (golden) raisins

1–2 large baking sheets, lined with baking parchment

Serves 10–12

Preheat the oven to 140°C (275°F) Gas 1.

Put the maple syrup, honey and oil in a small saucepan and set over low heat to warm through. Put the oats, nuts, seeds and salt in a large mixing bowl and stir well. Pour over the warmed syrup and mix thoroughly with a wooden spoon. All the oats must be moistened.

Spread the granola over the prepared baking sheets, making sure it is no deeper than 1 cm/½ inch, and bake in the preheated oven for 20 minutes.

Remove the sheets from the oven and stir the toasted, golden granola from the edges to the middle, then smooth out again. Return to the oven for a further 15–20 minutes, until lightly golden. Don't expect it to become crunchy — the mixture will remain soft until it cools.

Remove from the oven and let cool for 10 minutes before stirring in the raisins. Let cool completely, then break into pieces. Store in an airtight container and eat within 1 month.

Honey & Apricot Muffins

These deliciously wholesome muffins are a fantastic grab-and-go breakfast and contain plenty of dried fruit, nuts and other good things to keep your energy levels high all morning. They smell wonderful whilst baking and are best served fresh but will keep for 3–4 days in an airtight container.

200 g/1½ cups plain/all-purpose flour

½ teaspoon bicarbonate of soda/ baking soda

2½ teaspoons baking powder

2 teaspoons mixed/apple pie spice

50 g/½ cup chopped dried apricots

50 g/½ cup pecan nuts, chopped

100 g/1 cup porridge oats

50 g/½ cup (golden) raisins

2 bananas (preferably soft)

2 unpeeled apples, grated

2 eggs

5 tablespoons vegetable oil

1 teaspoon vanilla extract

4 tablespoons honey

6 tablespoons milk

100 g/½ cup light brown sugar

a 12-hole muffin pan, lined with muffin cases/liners

Makes 12

Preheat the oven to 180°C (350°F) Gas 4.

Sift the flour into a mixing bowl. Add the bicarbonate of soda/baking soda, baking powder and mixed/apple pie spice and stir to combine. Add the dried apricots, pecans and oats to the flour mixture together with the (golden) raisins and set aside.

In a separate bowl, mash the bananas with a fork. Add the apples, eggs, oil, vanilla extract, honey and milk and stir to combine. Add the sugar and stir again. Make a well in the middle of the dry ingredients. Pour in the wet ingredients and gently stir from the middle, gradually drawing in the dry ingredients to make a smooth batter. Do not overmix.

Fill the muffin cases/liners two thirds full and top with chopped pecans for added texture.

Bake in the top half of the preheated oven for approximately 30–40 minutes until the muffins are well risen, golden and springy to touch. Remove from the oven and cool on a wire rack then serve with cups of hot coffee.

Dairy-free Coconut Pancakes with Lime Syrup & Mango

These pancakes are completely dairy free; they don't even contain egg. This makes them a bit dense but as they are drenched in a lime syrup, this is soon taken care of.

150 g/1 cup plus 2 tablespoons plain/all-purpose flour

3 teaspoons baking powder

¼ teaspoon salt

2 tablespoons demerara sugar

3 tablespoons desiccated coconut

200 ml/¾ cup coconut milk

2 tablespoons sunflower oil, plus extra for frying

1 mango, peeled, pitted and sliced

Lime syrup

juice of 3 limes

grated zest of 1 lime

100 g/½ cup (clear) honey

6 cardamom pods, crushed

Serves 4

Preheat the oven to low.

To make the lime syrup, put the lime juice and zest, honey and cardamom pods in a small saucepan and bring to the boil. Boil for 5 minutes, then remove from the heat and set aside.

Meanwhile, sift the flour, baking powder and salt into a large mixing bowl and stir in the sugar and desiccated coconut. Put the coconut milk, 75 ml/⅓ cup water and the oil in another bowl and beat to combine. Mix the wet ingredients with the dry ingredients until no lumps of flour remain.

Heat a heavy-based frying pan/skillet over medium heat. Grease the pan with kitchen paper/paper towel dipped in oil. Drop 2–3 tablespoons of batter into the pan. Cook for 1–2 minutes on each side until golden and cooked through. Keep warm in the oven while you make the rest. Serve with mango and lime syrup.

Blueberry Pancakes

Perfect blueberry pancakes should be light and fluffy, with a good rise on them. The secret is to use some water – an all-milk batter makes the pancakes heavier. And remember to serve them with lashings of maple syrup.

125 g/1 cup self-raising/rising flour

1 teaspoon baking powder

2 tablespoons caster/granulated sugar

¼ teaspoon salt

1 egg

100 ml/⅓ cup whole milk

50 g/3 tablespoons butter, melted

150 g/1 generous cup blueberries, plus extra

maple syrup, to serve

Serves 4

Preheat the oven to low.

Sift the flour and baking powder into a large mixing bowl and stir in the sugar and salt. Put the egg, milk and 75 ml/⅓ cup water in another bowl and beat to combine.

Stir half the butter into the wet ingredients in the bowl. Mix the wet ingredients with the dry ingredients until no lumps of flour remain.

Wipe a heavy-based frying pan/skillet with scrunched-up kitchen paper/paper towel dipped in the remaining melted butter. Heat up, then drop in 4 tablespoons of the batter. Cook for 1–2 minutes on the first side, then scatter over a few of the blueberries and flip the pancake over. Cook for 2 minutes, until golden and cooked through. Keep warm in the oven while you make the rest. Serve with more blueberries and lashings of maple syrup.

Baked Tomatoes, Goats' Cheese & Herbs

Use quite a strong aged goats' cheese for this simple breakfast or brunch dish, as it contrasts against the sweetness of the tomatoes when they are cooked.

4 large stuffing tomatoes such as Marmande or heirloom, or more of a smaller variety
2 tablespoons extra virgin olive oil, plus extra to drizzle
1 onion, finely chopped
1 tablespoon chopped fresh thyme
200 g/6½ oz. goats' cheese
4 tablespoons dried breadcrumbs
2 eggs, beaten
a handful of fresh basil leaves

Serves 4

Preheat the oven to 180°C (350°F) Gas 4.

Slice the top third off the tomatoes and reserve. Using a melon baller, scoop out the seeds and juices and discard or reserve for making a tomato sauce.

Heat the oil in a frying pan/skillet, add the onion and thyme and soften for 5 minutes. Allow to cool slightly.

In a mixing bowl, beat the goats' cheese, breadcrumbs and eggs together and season well. Stir in the onion mixture and a few of the basil leaves. Divide the stuffing between the hollow tomatoes and top with the reserved tomato hats. Arrange in a baking dish, drizzle with oil and scatter over the remaining basil leaves. Bake in the preheated oven for 18–20 minutes.

Eggs Benedict

This dish is all about timing. Get everything ready before you cook the eggs and you won't have to rush

4 large eggs
2 whole-grain muffins, halved horizontally
8 slices of thin-cut ham
freshly ground black pepper

Hollandaise Sauce
2 tablespoons white wine vinegar
1 shallot, roughly chopped
½ teaspoon black peppercorns
2 large egg yolks
120 g/½ cup unsalted butter

Serves 4

Preheat the grill/broiler.

To make the hollandaise sauce, put the vinegar, 2 tablespoons cold water, the shallot and peppercorns in a saucepan and simmer over low heat for a few minutes until you have 1 tablespoon liquid remaining. Strain into a blender (or in a bowl if you are going to use an electric handheld whisk) with the egg yolks and set aside. Melt the butter in the same pan.

Fill a large, deep frying pan with water and bring to a simmer. Crack the eggs around the edge so they don't touch and poach for exactly 3 minutes. Meanwhile, put the muffins (cut side up) and ham on a baking sheet. Grill/broil for 2–3 minutes.

To finish the sauce, blend the eggs and vinegar until frothy. With the motor still running, add the melted butter in a very slow trickle until the sauce is thick. You should take about a minute to add all the butter. Any quicker and it will not emulsify.

Drape 2 slices of ham on top of each muffin half. Scoop out each poached egg and add to the stack. Pour over the hollandaise sauce and sprinkle with a grinding of black pepper.

Huevos Rancheros

You can buy cans of refried beans but it is just as easy to mash your own. If you want to serve this dish with a spoonful of guacamole, fresh salsa or sour cream, that's a great idea.

3 tablespoons vegetable oil

1 green chilli or jalapeño pepper, chopped

2 garlic cloves, crushed

500 g/1 lb. tomatoes, cut into slim wedges

400-g/14-oz. can pinto or cannellini beans

50 g/½ cup grated sharp cheddar

juice of 1 lime, plus extra lime wedges to serve

a handful of fresh coriander/cilantro leaves, chopped

4 eggs

4 corn tortillas

sea salt and freshly ground black pepper

Serves 4

Heat 1 tablespoon of the oil in a large frying pan/skillet over medium heat, then add the chilli, half the garlic and a pinch of salt and fry for 1–2 minutes, until softened. Add the tomatoes and cook gently for about 20 minutes.

Heat the remaining oil in a small saucepan, add the remaining garlic and heat through for 20 seconds, until just browning. Add the beans, then using a potato masher, coarsely mash the beans and stir in plenty of salt and pepper and the cheddar.

Stir the lime juice and coriander/cilantro into the tomato sauce. Make 4 holes in the sauce and crack an egg into each one. Cook for 3 minutes until set. Cover with the lid for the last 30 seconds just to firm up the whites.

Meanwhile, heat a frying pan/skillet over medium heat. Cook the tortillas for 1 minute on each side, until golden and hot. Transfer to 4 plates and spread the beans over the tortillas. Top with tomato salsa and the eggs. Serve with lime wedges and guacamole or sour cream.

Steak & Fried Egg Sandwiches

You need to eat this sandwich quickly before the egg has time to trickle down your chin.

100 g/7 tablespoons butter, soft

2 teaspoons wholegrain mustard

½ teaspoon English mustard powder

1 tablespoon chopped fresh tarragon
  leaves

1 teaspoon Gentleman's relish or
  anchovy paste (optional)

2 white buns, halved horizontally

2 x 250-g/8-oz. rib-eye or sirloin steaks,
  roughly 1.5 cm/⅝ inch thick

3 tablespoons olive oil

2 large eggs

sea salt and freshly ground black pepper

Serves 2

Put the butter in a mixing bowl and beat it with a spoon until squished against the sides of the bowl. Spoon in the wholegrain mustard, mustard powder, tarragon and relish, if using. Season to taste, taking care not to over-season as the relish will already be salty. Beat everything together and use to butter the insides of the buns.

Heat a ridged stovetop grill pan over high heat until very hot. Brush the steaks with 1 tablespoon of the oil and season. Using tongs, lay the steaks on the pan and press down. Let them cook for 2–4 minutes on each side. Press the middle of the steak to determine how well cooked it is. A light yield means it is medium, while anything soft is still rare. Transfer the steaks to a board and cut off any large pieces of fat. Let rest for 2–3 minutes while you cook the eggs.

Add the remaining oil to a frying pan/skillet and heat over high heat. Crack in the eggs and turn the heat to low. Cook for 2 minutes, then flip over for 30 seconds to cook the other side, but leave the yolk with a bit of ooze. Place a steak in each bun and finish off with a fried egg.

English Breakfast Quiche

Here are all the flavours of a traditional full farmhouse English fry-up in a quiche.

Pastry

225 g/1¾ cups plain/all-purpose flour

1 teaspoon English mustard powder

150 g/10 tablespoons butter, chilled
  and cubed

1 egg, beaten

Filling

4 pork sausages

200 g/6½ oz. cherry tomatoes, halved

200 g/6½ oz. bacon, cubed

200 g/6½ oz. button mushrooms, halved

1 tablespoon olive oil

300 ml/1¼ cups crème fraîche

3 large eggs, beaten

1 teaspoon English mustard powder

25-cm/10-inch fluted, loose-bottomed
  tart pan

baking beans

Serves 6

Preheat the oven to 200°C (400°F) Gas 6.

To make the pastry, put the flour, mustard powder and butter in a food processor and pulse until they are just combined. Add the egg and run the motor until the mixture just comes into a ball. Turn out, wrap with clingfilm/plastic wrap and refrigerate for 30 minutes.

To make the filling, put the sausages in a roasting pan and roast in the preheated oven for 10 minutes. Take the pan out of the oven, throw in the tomatoes, bacon and mushrooms, drizzle over the oil and return to the oven to roast for 15–20 minutes, until everything is tender and cooked through. Leave the oven on.

Roll out the pastry on a lightly floured surface until it is about 3 mm/⅛ inch thick and use to line the tart pan. Press the pastry into the corners and leave the overhang. Prick the base with a fork, line with baking parchment and fill with baking beans. Bake in the oven for 8 minutes, then remove the beans and paper. Trim off the overhang and reduce the heat to 150°C (300°F) Gas 2. Return the pastry case to the oven for 2–3 minutes to dry out.

To finish the filling, slice the sausages and scatter them with the rest of the roasted ingredients into the pastry case. Mix the crème fraîche, eggs and mustard powder and pour over everything in the pastry case. Bake for 30–35 minutes, until set around the edges. Turn off the oven and let the tart cool in the oven, with the door open, for 15 minutes. Cut into slices and serve warm or cold.

Baked Beans with Maple Syrup & Paprika

These homemade baked beans are utterly delicious. They are sweet and smoky and so irresistible. Pile on toasted and buttered whole-grain bread, or served with some hash browns.

2 x 400-g cans haricot/soldier, white navy or pinto beans, or 400 g/14 oz. dried beans
2 tablespoons butter
250 g/8 oz. (streaky) bacon or pancetta
2 onions, chopped
1 teaspoon smoked paprika
2 teaspoons Dijon mustard
1 tablespoon tomato purée
250 ml/1 cup hot stock
6 tablespoons maple syrup
sea salt and freshly ground black pepper

Serves 4

If using dried beans, put them in large bowl. Add enough water to cover by 8 cm/3 inches and let stand overnight. The next day, drain the beans and put them in a saucepan of water. Bring to the boil and simmer for 40 minutes until tender. Drain.

Preheat the oven to 150°C (300°F) Gas 2.

Heat the butter in a large ovenproof casserole dish and fry the bacon until it has browned. Add the onions, paprika and mustard. Reduce the heat to low, cover with a lid and cook for 5 minutes, stirring occasionally.

Add the cooked or canned beans, tomato purée, stock and some seasoning. Cover with a lid and bake in the preheated oven for 2 hours.

Give everything a good stir, add the maple syrup and taste to check the seasoning. Bake for a further 20 minutes with the lid off until the sauce has thickened. Serve with hot buttered toast or Hash Browns (see below).

Hash Browns

These hash browns are deep fried, which means you probably won't be making them every day. If you need to keep them warm while you cook the rest of your breakfast, pop them in the oven but put them on a wire rack first so they don't go soggy.

2 tablespoons butter
1 onion, chopped
600 g/1¼ lbs. large potatoes, peeled and grated
1 egg white, beaten
vegetable oil, for deep-frying
sea salt and freshly ground black pepper

Makes 16

Heat the butter in a frying pan/skillet, then add the onion, cover with a lid and cook over low heat until soft.

Put the potatoes into a large mixing bowl and stir in the softened onions. Stir in the egg white and season generously.

Fill a large saucepan one-third full with vegetable oil. Heat to 190°C/375°F (or until a blob of the potato mixture browns within a few seconds).

Roll the potato mixture into walnut-sized balls, then flatten slightly before adding to the hot oil. Fry in batches of 4–5 for 2–3 minutes, until golden brown. Drain on kitchen paper/paper towels and serve with extra salt, for sprinkling.

Soups & Small Bites

Smoky Chorizo & Bean Soup

This beautifully coloured soup is quick to cook and makes a warming lunch dish.

2 tablespoons olive oil

200 g/7 oz. chorizo sausage

1 red onion, thinly sliced

2 garlic cloves, chopped

¼ teaspoon Spanish smoked sweet paprika (pimentón dulce)

400-g/14-oz. can chopped tomatoes

500 ml/2 cups chicken or vegetable stock

410-g/14-oz. can haricot/navy beans, drained and well rinsed

a handful each of fresh flat leaf parsley and fresh coriander/cilantro leaves, roughly chopped

toasted baguette slices, rubbed with garlic, to serve

Serves 4

Heat the oil in a large saucepan set over high heat. Add the chorizo, onion and garlic and cook for 5 minutes, until the chorizo has browned and the onion has softened.

Stir in the paprika for 1 minute, until aromatic. Add the tomatoes, stock and beans and bring to the boil. Reduce the heat to a medium simmer and cook, uncovered, for 10 minutes. Stir in the parsley and coriander/cilantro and serve with garlic toasts.

Vegetarian option: Replace the chorizo with 400 g/2 cups sliced mushrooms and cook as you would the chorizo. Be sure to use vegetable stock and stir through a few handfuls of baby spinach leaves until wilted for some extra flavour.

Creamy Cannellini, Leek & Sorrel Soup

The sharp, lemon flavour of sorrel works well with the pleasingly smooth and creamy texture of cannellini beans.

50 g/3 tablespoons butter

1 leek, trimmed and sliced

2 garlic cloves, chopped

100 g/3 rashers/slices (streaky) bacon, thinly sliced

2 boiling potatoes (such as Desirée), diced

1 litre/4 cups vegetable or chicken stock

410-g/14-oz. can cannellini beans, drained and well rinsed

1 bunch sorrel, thinly sliced

125 ml/½ cup double/heavy cream

a handful of fresh flat leaf parsley leaves, finely chopped

sea salt and freshly ground black pepper

Serves 4

Heat the butter in a large saucepan set over medium heat. When the butter is sizzling, add the leek, garlic and bacon and cook for 10 minutes, until the leek is softened and silky looking and the bacon is golden.

Add the potatoes, stock and beans and bring to the boil. Reduce the heat to a medium simmer and cook for about 20 minutes, until the potatoes are tender. Stir in the sorrel and cook for a further 5 minutes, until the sorrel has wilted. Stir in the cream and season to taste with salt and pepper. Scatter the parsley over the top and serve.

Vegetarian option: Simply omit the bacon and use vegetable stock for a satisfying meat-free soup.

Creamy Tomato & Bread Soup with Basil Oil

This Italian soup is only as good as its ingredients — great tomatoes, good bread and wonderful, green olive oil. This is a great recipe for using up leftover bread — here it thickens the creamy tomato soup, which is in turn enriched with a generous amount of Parmesan. Learning to make your own herb oils is fun, too.

1.5 litres/6 cups vegetable, chicken or meat stock

4 tablespoons extra virgin olive oil

1 onion, peeled and chopped

1.2 kg/2½ lb. very ripe, soft tomatoes, chopped

300 g/10 oz. stale white bread, crusts removed and thinly sliced or made into breadcrumbs

3 cloves garlic, peeled and crushed

125 g/2 cups freshly grated Parmesan cheese, plus extra to serve

sea salt and freshly ground black pepper

Basil and rocket/arugula oil

150 ml/⅔ cup extra virgin olive oil

3 tablespoons chopped fresh basil

3 tablespoons chopped fresh rocket/arugula

Serves 6

Heat the stock slowly in a large saucepan. Meanwhile, heat the oil in a large saucepan and add the onion and tomatoes and fry over a gentle heat for 10 minutes until soft. Push the mixture through a food mill, mouli or sieve, and stir into the stock. Add the bread and garlic. Cover and simmer gently for about 45 minutes until thick and creamy, giving a good whisk every now and then to break up the bread. Watch out, as this soup can catch on the bottom.

Meanwhile, to make the basil and rocket/arugula oil, process the olive oil, basil and rocket/arugula in a blender until completely smooth and pour through a fine strainer, if necessary.

Stir the Parmesan into the soup and season with salt and pepper to taste. Ladle into bowls and trickle with 2 tablespoons basil and rocket/arugula oil and serve hot, warm or cold (but never chilled). Serve extra Parmesan separately.

Pork & Chicken Liver Terrine with Pistachios

A terrine is perfect for sharing. It can also be made well in advance and, once served up, there is no fuss. Simply lay out some good bread and dishes of pickles.

1 kg/2 ¼ lbs. minced/ground pork

200 g/7 oz. dry-cured pork lardons/trimmed and diced salt pork

300 g/10 oz. chicken livers, roughly chopped

1 garlic clove, crushed

finely grated zest of 1 orange

2 teaspoons fennel seeds

50 g/⅓ cup pistachios

1 egg, beaten

a handful of fresh flat leaf parsley leaves, finely chopped

12 bacon rashers/slices

cornichons (baby gherkins) and any sweet pickle, to serve

1 baguette, to serve

a loaf pan or terrine dish, 20 x 10 x 7 cm/ 8 x 4 x 3 inches, lightly oiled

a large, shallow baking dish or roasting pan

Serves 10–12

Put the minced/ground pork, lardons/salt pork, chicken livers, garlic, grated orange peel, fennel seeds and pistachios in a mixing bowl. Use your hands to combine thoroughly. Cover and refrigerate for at least 6 hours, preferably overnight, mixing occasionally.

Preheat the oven to 180°C (350°F) Gas 4.

Add the egg to the pork mixture and use your hands to thoroughly combine. Use the bacon to line the loaf pan, ensuring that the ends of the slices overhang the sides of the pan.

Spoon the pork mixture into the loaf pan, pressing it down into the pan. The filling may be higher than the top of the pan at this stage, but it will settle during cooking. Cover the top of the loaf pan firmly with 2 layers of foil. Put the pan in the large, shallow baking dish. Add enough hot water to come halfway up the sides of the loaf pan. Cook in the preheated oven for 3 hours.

Remove the terrine from the baking dish and let it cool completely, leaving the foil intact. When cool, remove the foil and carefully turn the terrine out onto a serving plate or board. Cover and refrigerate until ready to enjoy. Serve with the pickles and sliced baguette.

Smoked Mackerel & Lemon Pâté

A wonderfully quick pâté using smoked mackerel or any other moist smoked fish, this makes a simple yet impressive and delicious start to a dinner party or a tasty lunch.

250 g/8 oz. smoked mackerel fillets, skinned

rind of 1 small preserved lemon, finely chopped

3 tablespoons finely chopped fresh dill

250 g/8 oz. cream cheese, softened

300 g/10 oz. cherry tomatoes

1 tablespoon harissa

6–8 ramekins

Serves 6–8

Remove any stray bones from the mackerel fillets, then flake the mackerel into a bowl and mix with the preserved lemon, dill and cream cheese. Cover and refrigerate until ready to serve.

In a small serving bowl, combine the cherry tomatoes and harissa, crushing the tomatoes lightly with the back of a fork.

Divide the pâté between the ramekins and serve with the harissa crushed tomatoes.

Slow-cooked Tomatoes with Goats' Cheese & Garlic Toasts

Try to use in-season tomatoes for a sweet, heady flavour that works well with the tartness of the goats' cheese. These toasts are perfect to serve with drinks.

500 ml/2 cups extra virgin olive oil

1 sprig of fresh oregano

2 teaspoons finely chopped fresh flat leaf parsley leaves

6 very ripe Roma tomatoes

½ teaspoon sea salt

200 g/7 oz. soft goats' cheese

1 small baguette

2 garlic cloves, peeled

Serves 4

Preheat the oven to 130°C (250°F) Gas ½.

Put the oil in a small, non-reactive baking dish. Add the oregano and parsley. Cut the tomatoes in half and arrange them in a single layer in the dish. Ideally you want the tomatoes to be almost fully submerged in the oil. Sprinkle the salt evenly over the tomatoes. Cook in the preheated oven for about 5 hours, until the tomatoes are intensely red and softened yet still retain their shape. Remove from the oven and leave the tomatoes in the oil to cool completely.

Put the goats' cheese in a serving bowl. Preheat the grill/broiler. Slice the baguette very thinly. Toast the bread on both sides until golden and crisp and rub one side with the peeled garlic cloves.

Remove the tomatoes from the oil and arrange them on a serving platter with the cheese and garlic toasts on the side.

Roasted Red Pepper & Walnut Dip

This is a traditional Syrian dip called muhammara, often served in a meze selection. It also works well as a spooning sauce to serve with baked or grilled fish or lamb.

3 large red (bell) peppers

1 slice of day-old sourdough bread, cut into small pieces

100 g/⅔ cup walnut halves, coarsely chopped

½ teaspoon dried chilli/red pepper flakes

1 tablespoon sun-dried tomato paste

2 garlic cloves, chopped

2 teaspoons freshly squeezed lemon juice

1 tablespoon balsamic vinegar

2 teaspoons sugar

1 teaspoon ground cumin

2 tablespoons olive oil

chopped pistachios, to sprinkle

sea salt and freshly ground black pepper

toasted flatbread, roughly torn, to serve

Serves 6–8

Cook the peppers one at a time by skewering each one on a fork and holding it directly over a gas flame for 10–15 minutes, until the skin is blackened all over. Alternatively, put them on a baking tray and then in an oven preheated to 220°C (425°F) Gas 7. Cook them for about 10–15 minutes, until the skin has puffed up and blackened all over. Transfer to a bowl, cover with a tea towel and leave until cool enough to handle.

Using your hands, remove the skin and seeds from the peppers and tear the flesh into pieces. (Avoid rinsing with water, as this will remove the smoky flavour.) Put it in a food processor and add the remaining ingredients. Process to a coarse paste. Season to taste with salt and pepper and transfer to a bowl. Cover with clingfilm/plastic wrap and refrigerate for at least 8 hours to allow the flavours to develop.

To serve, bring the dip to room temperature and transfer it to a shallow bowl. Drizzle with olive oil and sprinkle with chopped pistachios. Serve with torn toasted flatbreads. It will keep in an airtight container in the refrigerator for 4–5 days.

Dolmades with Green Lentils, Currants & Herbs

These are vine leaves wrapped around a tasty mixture of rice, herbs and nuts.

200-g/7-oz. jar vine/grape leaves

1 tablespoon olive oil

1 small onion, finely chopped

165 g/⅔ cup short grain (pudding) rice

45 g/¼ cup dried green lentils

125 ml/½ cup chicken or vegetable stock

2 tablespoons currants

50 g/⅓ cup lightly toasted pine nuts

2 tablespoons finely chopped fresh mint

2 tablespoons finely chopped fresh flat leaf parsley

2 tablespoons finely chopped fresh dill

65 ml/¼ cup extra virgin olive oil

2 tablespoons freshly squeezed lemon juice

sea salt and freshly ground black pepper

Makes 24

To prepare the vine/grape leaves, separate the leaves and soak in cold water for about 15 minutes. Drain well and pat dry with paper towels.

Heat the 1 tablespoon oil in a small saucepan set over high heat and cook the onion for 2–3 minutes, until softened. Stir in the rice and lentils for 1 minute. Add the stock, stir to combine and to remove any grains stuck to the bottom of the pan. Cover and cook over low heat for 10 minutes. Tip the mixture into a bowl and stir in the currants, pine nuts, mint, parsley and dill and season well.

Pick out 24 of the largest, least torn vine leaves. Use the remaining leaves to line the base of a large, heavy-based saucepan and pour over half of the extra virgin olive oil.

Lay a vine/grape leaf, vein-side down, on a work surface. Put 1 tablespoon of the filling in the centre of the leaf and fold the stalk end over, bringing the sides in as you roll to enclose the filling. Do not roll up too firmly, as the rice will expand and cause the leaves to split. Repeat to use all the filling. Pack the dolmades into the saucepan, so they fit snugly in one layer. Pour over the remaining oil, lemon juice and 500 ml/2 cups cold water. Gently bring to the boil then reduce heat to low simmer. Cover with an inverted plate and cook over low heat for 45 minutes. Remove from the heat and let sit in the pan for a few minutes and when cool enough to handle, remove from the pan and serve.

Spicy Masala Kale Chips

Kale chips are a healthier alternative to processed crunchy snack foods like potato chips.

1 head of curly kale or 1 bag of pre-chopped curly kale (about 50 g/1¾ oz.)

1 large tomato, quartered

3 sun-dried tomatoes (dry not marinated ones, with no added sugar)

½ teaspoon paprika

¼ teaspoon ground cumin

a pinch of sea salt

⅛–¼ teaspoon cayenne pepper

freshly ground black pepper

baking sheet lined with foil

Serves 2–4

Preheat the oven to 200°C (400°F) Gas 6.

Tear small pieces of kale off the stems and place them in a colander. Wash them, then dry as thoroughly as possible. Place the dry pieces in a large bowl.

Put the tomato quarters and sun-dried tomatoes in a food processor. Pulse until smooth, scraping down the sides of the bowl as you go. It won't seem like a lot of mixture, but the idea is just to flavour the kale rather than cover it in a thick sauce. Add the paprika, cumin and salt, then as much cayenne and black pepper as you like, depending on how spicy you want your chips to turn out. Process the mixture again, then pour it into the bowl of kale. Using your hands, toss the kale so that it is evenly coated in the masala mixture.

Spread the kale onto the prepared baking sheet. Bake in the preheated oven with the door slightly ajar for 14–16 minutes. The kale is ready when it is crispy and thin. If you can resist eating it immediately, store in an airtight container for 4–5 days at room temperature.

Salmon Rillettes with Melba Toast

A rillette is a very traditional way of potting and preserving meats, such as pork or duck in fat. Here is a lighter, healthier and fuss-free version of this French classic.

300 g/10 oz. salmon fillet (smoked if liked), skinned and pin-boned

50 g/3 tablespoons unsalted butter, chilled and cut into cubes

½ teaspoon sea salt

1 lemon, 1 half sliced and the other juiced

1 tablespoon finely chopped fresh dill

2 tablespoons snipped fresh chives

4 slices of white bread

Serves 4

Preheat the oven to 220°C (425°F) Gas 7.

Put the salmon on a sheet of baking parchment large enough to wrap the fish entirely. Distribute the butter cubes evenly over the fish, sprinkle with the sea salt, add the lemon slices and finish with the dill. Firmly wrap up the fish in the paper, put it on a baking sheet and cook in the preheated oven for 10 minutes. Leave in the paper and let cool to room temperature.

Remove the fish from the paper and pour any collected oil and juices into a large bowl. Discard the lemon slices. Flake the fish and put it in the bowl with the juices then add the chives and the lemon juice. Cover and refrigerate until needed.

To make the Melba toasts, preheat the grill to high and trim the crusts off the bread. Toast the bread on both sides until golden. Using a serrated knife, carefully cut each slice widthways to make 8 very thin slices. Cut each slice into 4 small triangles, return these to the grill and toast the uncooked side until golden. Serve alongside the salmon rillettes.

Chilli Salt Squid

Fresh squid can look a little scary, but it really is superior to the frozen stuff. Cook it in one of two ways: very quickly or for a long time – anywhere in between makes it tough.

400 g/14 oz. cleaned squid (1 large tube)

2 tablespoons cornflour/cornstarch

1 tablespoon plain/all-purpose flour

½ teaspoon ground white pepper

½ teaspoon mild chilli powder

3 teaspoons sea salt

1 large red chilli, thinly sliced

a small handful of fresh coriander/cilantro leaves, chopped

vegetable oil, for deep-frying

lemon wedges, to serve

Serves 4

Cut the squid tube down one side so that it opens up. Use a sharp knife to trim and discard any internal membranes. Cut it lengthways into 2-cm/1-inch wide strips, then cut each strip in half. Combine the flours, pepper, chilli powder and salt in a large bowl. Half-fill a saucepan with the vegetable oil and heat over high heat until the surface of the oil shimmers.

Toss half of the squid pieces in the flour mixture, quickly shaking off the excess, and add them to the oil. Cook for about 2 minutes, until deep golden. Remove with a slotted spoon and drain on kitchen paper/paper towels. Repeat with the remaining squid. Add the chilli slices to the oil and cook for just a few seconds. Remove from the pan and drain on kitchen paper/paper towels. Put the squid and chilli on a serving plate and sprinkle with the coriander/cilantro. Serve while still warm with plenty of lemon wedges on the side for squeezing.

Sesame Prawn Toasts

This prawn mixture can be 'prepped' several hours in advance – perfect for entertaining.

300 g/10 oz. raw peeled and deveined
   prawns/shrimp
6 spring onions/scallions, finely chopped
1 tablespoon finely grated fresh ginger
2 teaspoons dry sherry (optional)
1 teaspoon light soy sauce
1 egg white, lightly beaten
6 thick slices of white bread
50 g/½ cup sesame seeds
sea salt
about 250 ml/about 1 cup vegetable oil,
   for shallow frying
sprigs of fresh coriander/cilantro,
   to garnish

Pickled carrot

1 large carrot, coarsely grated
2 tablespoons Japanese pickled ginger,
   sliced
2 tablespoons juice from the pickled
   ginger jar
½ teaspoon sugar
2 shallots, thinly sliced on the diagonal

Makes 24 toasts

To make the pickled carrot, combine the carrot, pickled ginger, pickled ginger juice, sugar and shallots in a small, non-reactive bowl. Set aside until needed.

Put the prawns/shrimp, spring onions/scallions, ginger, sherry, soy sauce, egg white and some salt in a food processor. Process until roughly chopped.

Trim the crusts off the bread and discard or save for another use. Cut each slice into 4 triangles. Put the sesame seeds on a plate. Spread about 2 teaspoons of the prawn/shrimp mixture onto each piece of bread, pressing down lightly. Press each triangle into the sesame seeds to lightly coat.

Put the oil in a shallow frying pan/skillet and heat over medium/high heat. Add a piece of bread to test if the oil is ready – if the bread sizzles on contact, the oil is hot enough. Use a fish slice to carefully add the prawn/shrimp toasts to the pan, prawn/shrimp-side down, and cook for 1 minute. Turn over and cook for 1 minute more, until golden. Drain on kitchen paper/paper towels. Spoon a little pickled carrot over the top of each toast and add a sprig of coriander/cilantro. Serve immediately.

Pancetta & Fennel Puffs

These are a type of savoury doughnut flavoured with diced pancetta and fennel seeds.

about 200 ml/¾ cup milk, warmed
50 g/¼ cup lard
40 g/1.5 oz. fresh yeast or 1 sachet fast-
   action dried yeast
400 g/3 cups plain/all-purpose white flour
50 g/2 oz. pancetta, finely diced
1 teaspoon fennel seeds, chopped
vegetable or olive oil, for deep-frying
sea salt

a deep-fryer

Serves 8

Warm the milk with the lard. When melted, crumble in the fresh yeast, if using, and whisk until dissolved. Sift the flour with a good pinch of salt into a bowl and make a well in the centre. If using easy-blend dried yeast, stir it into the flour now. Pour in the warm milk and lard mixture, then add the pancetta and fennel seeds. Mix to a soft dough, adding more flour, if necessary. Form into a ball, cover and leave to rise for 2 hours or until doubled.

Heat the oil in the deep-fryer to 180°C (350°F) – a piece of stale bread dropped in should turn golden in a few seconds. Punch down the dough and knead for 1 minute. Pull off small walnut-sized pieces of dough, about 2 cm/1 inch, and roll into rough balls. Fry in batches for about 2–3 minutes until pale brown and puffy. Drain well and tip onto kitchen paper/paper towels. Sprinkle with salt and serve whilst still hot.

Blinis with Smoked Salmon & Crème Fraîche

It's worth making your own fresh blinis because their flavour is much more complex than the ready-made kind. You can make the batter the night before, then let it have its final rising half an hour before cooking. They freeze well too.

50 g/⅓ cup buckwheat flour plus
    50 g/½ cup strong plain/bread flour
1 teaspoon salt
125 ml/½ cup whole milk
75 ml/⅓ cup crème fraîche, plus extra
7 g/1 envelope dried active yeast
1 large egg, separated
sunflower oil, for frying
smoked salmon, to serve
snipped chives (optional)

Makes 20 small blinis

Sift the flours and salt into a large mixing bowl. Heat the milk in a saucepan until hand hot. Add the crème fraîche and yeast and stir until smooth. Pour onto the flours with the egg yolk and stir well to blend. Cover and let rise for 1 hour.

Beat the egg white with an electric handheld whisk until soft peaks form. Fold into the batter, cover and leave for 30 minutes. Preheat the oven to low.

To make the blinis, heat a heavy-based frying pan/skillet over medium heat. Grease with kitchen paper/paper towel dipped in oil. Drop in 2 tablespoons of the batter. After 30 seconds bubbles will appear on the surface. Flip the blini over and cook for 30 seconds on the other side. Keep warm in the oven while you cook the rest. Serve with crème fraîche, smoked salmon, chives, if using, and black pepper.

Smoked Salmon Brochettes

Who said party food had to be difficult and complicated? This simple idea can be prepared in the morning, covered with clingfilm/plastic wrap and refrigerated until just before serving (it will taste better if you let it come back to room temperature first).

250 g/8 oz. smoked salmon
finely grated zest of 2 lemons
freshly ground black pepper

Serves 12

Cut slices of smoked salmon lengthways into long strips, about 1 cm/½ inch wide and 10 cm/4 inches long. (Most slices will produce about 3 strips.) Thread the strips carefully onto cocktail sticks/toothpicks.

Arrange the loaded sticks on a serving platter and sprinkle with finely grated lemon zest and black pepper.

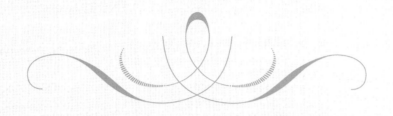

Salads
& Sides

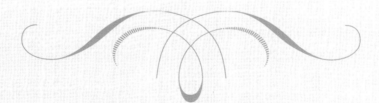

Greek Salad with Butter Beans

This is a slight twist on a classic Greek salad. Butter beans are a staple of Greek cuisine but are usually served baked in a rich tomato sauce and served as part of a meze. Their delicate flavour works well here with tangy feta and olives.

400 g/14 oz. cherry tomatoes, halved

50 g/½ cup kalamata olives, halved and pitted

leaves from a bunch of fresh mint, roughly chopped

leaves from a bunch of fresh parsley, finely chopped

2 x 410-g/14-oz. cans butter beans, drained

3 tablespoons olive oil

2 red onions, thinly sliced

2 garlic cloves, finely chopped

3 tablespoons freshly squeezed lemon juice

200 g/7 oz. feta cheese, cut into cubes

sea salt and freshly ground black pepper

bread, to serve

Serves 4

Put the tomatoes, olives, mint, parsley and beans in a large bowl and toss to combine.

Put the oil in a frying pan/skillet set over medium heat. Add the onions and garlic. When they start to sizzle in the oil, remove from the heat and pour over the tomato mixture. Stir in the lemon juice and add the feta. Season to taste with salt and pepper and toss well to combine. Serve at room temperature with bread.

Fresh Beans with Pecorino & Prosciutto

The contrast of fresh green-flavoured beans, creamy, salty cheese and fruity, salty meat in this salad is divine.

500 g/2 lbs. fresh young unshelled broad/fava beans, or 175 g/6 oz. frozen broad/fava beans, thawed

110 g/4 oz. young pecorino cheese

6 slices Italian dry-cured ham (prosciutto crudo)

5 tablespoons olive oil

2 tablespoons freshly squeezed lemon juice

2 teaspoons chopped fresh oregano

2 tablespoons chopped fresh flat leaf parsley

a pinch of dried chilli/hot pepper flakes (optional)

sea salt and freshly ground black pepper

Serves 4

Remove the broad/fava beans from their shells, blanch in boiling water for 20 seconds, drain and refresh, then pop them out of their skins and place in a bowl. If using frozen beans, thaw then pop them out of their skins and put in a bowl.

Cut the pecorino cheese into cubes and cut the ham into strips, then add to the beans. Whisk together the olive oil, lemon juice, oregano, parsley and pepper flakes, if using, and pour over the bean mixture. Toss together and season to taste with salt and pepper. Serve immediately.

Lentil & Artichoke Salad with Salsa Verde

This salsa verde is also delicious spooned over rare roast beef, grilled/broiled chicken, smoked salmon or grilled/broiled tuna steaks. The capers, anchovies and pickles have a long shelf life so don't be put off by the long list of ingredients.

200 g/1 cup Puy lentils

400 g/14 oz. chargrilled artichokes, quartered

Salsa verde

a handful of fresh mint leaves

a handful of fresh flat leaf parsley leaves

a handful of fresh basil leaves

2 teaspoons salted capers, rinsed

2 anchovy fillets in oil (optional)

2 garlic cloves

1 pickled gherkin (about 5 cm/2 inches long)

3 tablespoons olive oil

1 tablespoon red wine vinegar

2 teaspoons Dijon mustard

Serves 4

To make the salsa verde, put all the ingredients in a food processor and process until you have a chunky green sauce. Set aside.

Cook the lentils in a large saucepan of boiling water for about 30 minutes, until tender yet still firm to the bite. Drain well and transfer to a large bowl. Add the artichokes and stir in the salsa. Serve soon after making as the salsa will quickly lose its colour.

Pepper, Bean & Halloumi Salad

Halloumi turns rubbery soon after cooking so serve this salad as quickly as possible.

300 g/1½ cups dried black-eyed beans/cow peas

3 fresh plum tomatoes (such as Roma), diced

1 red (bell) pepper, deseeded and diced

leaves from a bunch of fresh coriander/cilantro, chopped

65 ml/¼ cup olive oil

200 g/7 oz. halloumi cheese, cut into 2.5 cm/1-inch pieces

2 tablespoons freshly squeezed lemon juice

1 tablespoon red wine vinegar

sea salt and freshly ground black pepper

Serves 4

Put the beans in a bowl, cover with cold water and let soak overnight.

Drain the beans and cook in a large saucepan of boiling water for 1–1½ hours, until tender. Drain and transfer to a large bowl. Add the tomatoes, red pepper, coriander/cilantro and half of the oil.

Heat the remaining oil in a non-stick frying pan/skillet set over high heat. Add the halloumi and cook for 3–4 minutes, turning often, until golden brown all over. Add to the bowl with the tomato mixture and stir in the lemon juice and vinegar. Season to taste and serve immediately.

Quinoa with New Season Beans, Peas & Asparagus

This recipe is a celebration of new-season spring vegetables, served with quinoa. The fresh, bright colours make the dish look so appealing.

300 g/1½ cups quinoa

2 teaspoons bouillon stock powder

12 asparagus spears, chopped in half

200 g/2 cups shelled broad/fava beans

200 g/2 cups peas

handful of cherry tomatoes, halved

large handful of fresh mint, roughly chopped

handful of fresh flat leaf parsley, roughly chopped

grated zest and juice of 1 lemon

200 ml/¾ cup extra virgin olive oil

2 tablespoons agave syrup

1 tablespoon pomegranate molasses (or balsamic vinegar)

sea salt and freshly ground black pepper

Serves 6

Put the quinoa and bouillon powder in a saucepan and cover with just under double its volume of water. Bring to the boil, then reduce the heat to low and place the lid on top. Cook for about 12 minutes until all the water has been absorbed. Turn off the heat, remove the lid and let any remaining water evaporate. Remove to a wide plate and allow to cool.

Meanwhile, bring a pan of water to the boil (just enough to cover each set of vegetables you are cooking) and add 2 teaspoons salt. Cook the asparagus, beans and peas separately until just tender – about 3–4 minutes for each. You still want them to have a bit of bite.

Once the beans are cooked, they need to have their outer cases removed. Simply slide the pale case off each bean and discard.

In a large bowl, gently but thoroughly mix the quinoa, asparagus, beans, peas, tomatoes and herbs, reserving some of the herbs for serving. Add the lemon zest and juice, oil, agave syrup, molasses, salt and pepper. Mix again, taste and check the seasoning. Serve in a large dish with the remaining herbs sprinkled on top. Finish with a drizzle of oil.

Chargrilled Asparagus

This simple dish makes the most of asparagus when fresh and in season, with the walnut mayonnaise adding an extra depth of flavour.

bunch of asparagus spears

extra virgin olive oil

grated zest of ½ lemon

small handful of walnuts

a little freshly chopped flat leaf parsley

sea salt

Walnut mayonnaise

300 ml/1¼ cups good extra virgin olive oil

300 ml/1¼ cups extra virgin olive oil

300 ml/1¼ cups walnut oil

2 egg yolks

squeeze of lemon juice

Serves 2–4

To make the walnut mayonnaise, you can use a food processor or an electric whisk. Either way, combine the oils in a jug/pitcher. Put the egg yolks, lemon juice and a pinch of salt in the food processor bowl or a mixing bowl. As you start to process/whisk, very slowly feed in the oils a little at a time until the mixture begins to emulsify and come together. Once this happens you can add the oil a bit faster, but never be tempted to fire it all in otherwise the mayonnaise will split. Refrigerate until needed.

Heat a stovetop grill pan over high heat. Snap the bases off the asparagus spears where they naturally break. Toss the asparagus in a few drops of oil so they are lightly coated.

Grill the asparagus for about 3 minutes depending on the thickness. Turn them now and again to get an even char. You want the asparagus to still retain a bit of bite.

Pile the asparagus up on a plate and scatter over some lemon zest and salt. Put a tablespoon of walnut mayonnaise on top, scatter over the walnuts and parsley and drizzle over olive oil.

Globe Artichokes with Fennel

This combination of ingredients makes a great side dish to serve with fish.

3 globe artichokes

bunch of fresh thyme

bunch of fresh oregano

3 fennel bulbs

2 lemons

2 tablespoons extra virgin olive oil, plus extra for drizzling

100 g/3½ oz. rocket/arugula leaves

1 tablespoon freshly chopped flat leaf parsley

sea salt and freshly ground black pepper

Serves 4

Preheat the oven to 200°C (400°F) Gas 6. Fill a saucepan with enough water to just cover the artichokes (but don't add the artichokes yet) and bring to the boil. Cut the stalks off the artichokes leaving about 4 cm/1½ inches in length from the base. With a serrated knife, cut the top quarter of the artichoke off so you come down to the top of the choke. Pull off the outer tough leaves to reach the inner, pale leaves of the heart. Peel the outer layer of skin from the stalk and the base of the artichoke. Now cut the artichokes in half lengthways through the stalk and remove the prickly inner choke with a teaspoon. Have a lemon ready to squeeze over the skin in order to prevent it from discolouring.

Put the prepared artichokes, thyme, oregano and about 2 teaspoons of salt into the pan of boiling water. Reduce the heat a little and simmer until the artichokes are very tender and a sharp knife can be easily inserted. To keep the artichokes submerged and prevent them from discolouring, place a heatproof plate or lid directly on the surface of the water.

Cut the base and tops off the fennel and remove the tough outer layer. Cut into quarters, then toss with the oil. Season with salt and tip onto to a baking sheet. Peel the zest off 1 lemon in large pieces, cut the lemon in half, then add all of it to the fennel. Cover with foil and bake for 35 minutes or until quite soft. Remove the foil and roast for a further 10 minutes or until they colour a little. Once the vegetables are ready, grate the zest from the second lemon and add most of it to the vegetables with a drizzle of olive oil. Toss the leaves with the remaining lemon zest, the juice of half a lemon, some salt and oil. Scatter over the parsley and drizzle with more oil.

Basil, Mozzarella & Orzo Salad

This dish is full of rustic charm, delicious ingredients and fresh Italian flavours.

a large handful of fresh basil, roughly chopped

20 g/¼ cup finely grated Parmesan cheese

1 garlic clove

25 g/3 tablespoons toasted pine nuts, plus a few extra to garnish

1 tablespoon extra virgin olive oil

175 g/1 cup orzo pasta

150 g/5½ oz. buffalo mozzarella, torn

50 g/⅓ cup sun-blushed (semi-dried) tomatoes, roughly chopped

a handful of wild rocket/arugula

sea salt and freshly ground black pepper

Serves 2

In a blender, whizz up most of the basil (keep a few leaves back for garnish), the grated Parmesan, garlic, pine nuts, olive oil and a grind of salt and pepper to make a fresh pesto.

Bring a small pan of water to the boil, add the orzo and cook for 8 minutes or until al dente. Drain and refresh under cold running water before draining again.

In a large mixing bowl, combine the orzo and the pesto, mixing thoroughly, then add the torn mozzarella, chopped tomatoes and rocket/arugula and toss through. Lastly garnish with the last few sprigs of basil and a sprinkling of pine nuts before serving.

Ham Hock, Bean & Mint Salad with a Creamy Mustard Dressing

Ham hock, broad/fava beans, mint and mustard are a marriage made in flavour heaven and this salad is summer served on a plate. Keep the ham hock, herbs and pea shoots separate from the dressing until just before serving as the herbs and shoots tend to wilt.

750 g/1½ lb. Jersey Royal new potatoes, washed and left whole

750 g/1½ lb. fresh broad/fava beans

750 g/1½ lb. fresh peas

500 g/1 lb. mangetout/snow peas, trimmed

1 bunch of fresh flatleaf parsley, roughly chopped

2 tablespoons chopped fresh mint

180 g/6 oz. cooked ham hock meat, shredded

70 g/2 big handfuls of pea shoots, to garnish (optional)

sea salt and freshly ground black pepper

Creamy mustard dressing

3 tablespoons extra virgin olive oil

3 tablespoons white wine vinegar

a good pinch of sea salt

1 generous teaspoon French wholegrain mustard

1 teaspoon crème fraîche

1 banana shallot (or two small shallots) very finely diced

Serves 4–6

Bring a large saucepan of water to the boil, add the new potatoes and boil for 15–20 minutes until cooked through. Remove from heat, drain and leave to cool.

Add more water to the pan, bring to the boil again, then add the broad/fava beans and after 1 minute add the peas and mangetout/snow peas. Boil for a further 1 minute before draining, then transfer to a bowl of iced water to refresh. Drain all the peas and beans and put to one side.

For the dressing, put the olive oil and white wine vinegar in a large mixing bowl with a good pinch of salt, and beat with a fork to dissolve the salt in the vinegar. Add the mustard, crème fraîche and shallot and mix well again. Pop the mixed peas and beans and the new potatoes in the bowl with the dressing and mix well.

Just before serving, add the parsley, mint and ham hock to the dressed peas and beans and toss together. Season to taste with sea salt and ground black pepper, then sprinkle the pea shoots on top, to garnish, if using.

Cannellini Bean, Avocado & Mint

Using canned beans means that there is no cooking required in this dish. Simply mix the beans with the fresh ingredients for an instant plate of goodness.

2 x 400-g/14-oz. cans cannellini beans

2 large avocados

4 spring onions/scallions sliced on the diagonal

good handful of fresh mint leaves, torn if they are very big

1 garlic clove, crushed

grated zest and fresh juice of 1 lemon

4 tablespoons extra virgin olive oil

sea salt and freshly ground black pepper

Serves 4–6

Drain and rinse the beans and place in a bowl. Cut the avocados in half, remove the stones and spoon the flesh out of the skin. Slice lengthways and add to the bowl.

Add the spring onions/scallions, mint leaves, garlic, lemon zest and juice, and oil. Mix together and season to taste with salt and pepper. If it does not taste exciting, add more lemon zest, salt and oil.

Salad of Truffled French Beans

A truffle has one of those delicious subtle qualities that can really enhance a dish. You can buy preserved truffles in the specialist ingredients aisle of a supermarket or in fine foods delicatessens.

750 g/1½ lbs. new potatoes or baby potatoes

220 g/8 oz. French beans

1–2 tablespoons caper berries, drained

a handful of fresh tarragon leaves, roughly chopped

2 small preserved black summer truffles (optional)

sea salt and freshly ground black pepper

Truffle dressing

1 tablespoon white wine vinegar

1 tablespoon olive oil

1 teaspoon wholegrain mustard

2–3 teaspoons truffle oil

Serves 8

Bring the potatoes to the boil in a saucepan of salted water. After simmering for 8 minutes, add a steamer above the saucepan with the French beans and cook both the potatoes and beans for a further 3 minutes. (The potatoes should have a total of 10–11 minutes until they are cooked through.) Drain and refresh both the potatoes and beans under cold running water until completely cool, then dry off.

For the dressing, put the vinegar and olive oil in a jar or other sealable container, add a generous pinch of salt, the wholegrain mustard, black pepper and finish with the truffle oil, then shake together.

Toss together the beans and potatoes with the caper berries and tarragon. If you managed to find the black summer truffles, use a vegetable or truffle peeler to shave very thin slices over the salad and toss through. Season the salad with sea salt and black pepper and finally drizzle with truffle dressing just before serving.

Aubergine, Puy Lentils & Sun-dried Tomatoes with Mint Oil

With lentils it is all about the seasoning — lashings of olive oil, lemon juice and salt.

300 g/1½ cups Puy lentils (or other green lentils)

extra virgin olive oil

1 red onion, finely chopped

2 garlic cloves, crushed

450 ml/2 cups vegetable stock (or water with a carrot, ½ onion, celery stalk, dried bay leaf and thyme sprigs thrown into the lentils to make your own stock as they are cooking)

3 aubergines/eggplants, topped, tailed and cut into 1-cm/½-inch slices

grated zest of 1 lemon and juice of ½

100 g/⅔ cup sun-dried tomatoes

1 tablespoon agave syrup

1 tablespoon red wine vinegar

1 tablespoon dark soy sauce

a big handful of fresh mint leaves

sea salt and freshly ground black pepper

Serves 6

Wash and drain the lentils. Heat 2 tablespoons oil in a large, heavy-based casserole dish over medium heat. Turn down the heat, add the onion and fry gently until translucent but not coloured. Add the garlic and fry for 1 minute. Add the lentils and stir well. Pour the stock in and bring to the boil. Reduce the heat, simmer, then cover with the lid and cook for 25 minutes or until the lentils are tender and have absorbed most of the stock.

Meanwhile, heat a large, dry stovetop grill pan over medium heat until hot. Using a pastry brush, coat the aubergine/eggplant slices with oil on both sides. Place them on the pan and fry for a few minutes. Check they have gone a golden brown, then flip over and fry for another few minutes until golden. When cooked, they should be soft to the touch. Remove to a plate and season with salt. Drizzle over the agave syrup and plenty of oil. (The quality of the oil is key here — the aubergine soaks it all up so you will really be able to taste it.)

When the lentils are done, drain them of all but a few tablespoons of the cooking liquid. While still hot, season with the lemon zest and juice, vinegar, soy sauce and a few glugs of oil. Mix well and allow to cool slightly. Taste it when it is at room temperature and season if necessary. Mix in the tomatoes. Finely chop the mint leaves (reserve a few for serving) and combine with enough oil to make a dense mint oil. Nestle the aubergine/eggplant slices among the lentils, drizzle over the mint oil and scatter with the remaining mint.

Grated Carrots, Blood Orange & Walnuts

The colour of this blood orange salad is enough to win anyone over, but it is full of flavour as well. It's perfect as a side or with a number of other salads, all sumptuously laid out together. Get your hands on blood oranges while they are in season.

2 blood oranges

8 large carrots, grated

grated zest and juice of 1 lemon

3 tablespoons agave syrup

1 tablespoon freshly chopped flat leaf parsley

4 tablespoons extra virgin olive oil

2 handfuls of walnuts, fresh from the shell

sea salt

Serves 6

Cut the top and bottom off the oranges, just down to the flesh, then place the orange on its end, cut side down, and carefully, following the shape of the orange, cut the peel off in strips from top to bottom, making sure you cut off the white pith too. Then turn them on their side and cut them into 1-cm/⅜-inch thick rounds. Do this on a board or somewhere that will catch any orange juice that you inadvertently squeeze out of them; this can be added to the dish too.

Squeeze any excess juice out of the grated carrots to prevent the salad from being too soggy (you can drink any juice you extract). In a large bowl, combine the carrots with all the other ingredients. This should be a punchy, citrussy salad with just enough sweetness from the agave. Let all the flavours combine together for 15 minutes, then taste again, adjust the seasoning with more juice, parsley, salt and agave if necessary.

Roasted Vegetables

It takes just minutes to throw these vegetables and herbs in a roasting pan, then you can forget about them for 30 or 40 minutes while the heat of the oven brings out all their lovely flavours. These go with anything – fish, meat, rice or pasta.

1 red onion, cut into wedges

250 g/8 oz. courgettes/zucchini, sliced

225 g/7 oz. baby corn

225 g/7 oz. aubergine/eggplant, cut into large chunks

1 red (bell) pepper, deseeded and cut into large chunks

1 yellow pepper, deseeded and cut into large chunks

16 cherry tomatoes

2–4 garlic cloves, thinly sliced

1 red chilli, deseeded and chopped

1½ tablespoons olive oil

2 tablespoons chopped fresh basil leaves

1 tablespoon chopped fresh rosemary

balsamic vinegar, for drizzling

sea salt and freshly ground black pepper

Serves 6–8

Preheat the oven to 220°C (425°F) Gas 7.

Put the onion, courgettes/zucchini, corn, aubergine/eggplant, peppers, tomatoes, garlic and chilli, if using, in a large non-stick roasting pan. Sprinkle with the oil, season with salt and pepper and toss until all the vegetables are lightly coated with the oil. Don't be tempted to add any more oil as the vegetables will release plenty of juices when cooking. Shake the pan gently to make the vegetables lie in a single layer.

Roast in a preheated oven for 30–40 minutes, turning once or twice during cooking, until the vegetables are beginning to brown at the edges.

Remove from the oven, sprinkle with the basil and rosemary and toss well. Drizzle over a little balsamic vinegar and serve.

Roast Potatoes

Potatoes are the quintessential roast vegetable. The idea is to get a crisp, crunchy outside and a fluffy inside. If you score the outside of the potato first with a fork, they will be extra crunchy.

150 ml/⅔ cup double/heavy cream

½ teaspoon hot dry mustard

½ teaspoon salt

500 g/1 lb. potatoes, peeled and halved

Serves 4

Put the cream, mustard and salt in a measuring jug/pitcher and beat with a fork. Put the potatoes in a small roasting pan and pour the cream mixture over the top. Roast in a preheated oven at 180°C (350°F) Gas 4 for 1 hour, basting every 20 minutes. Serve with roast meat or poultry. The cream becomes buttery as it cooks – don't worry, it's going to turn brown and crumbly.

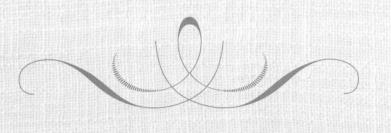

Just the
Two of Us

Pecorino, Pepper & Pig Cheek Pasta

Pure comfort food, this makes a great weekend dish when you have more time to cook.

1 tablespoon olive oil

125 g/4 oz. guanciale, lardons or bacon

1 onion, sliced into half moons

300 g/10 oz. (about 2) trimmed pig cheeks, cut into wine cork-sized chunks

1 tablespoon plain/all-purpose flour

1½ tablespoons ground black pepper, plus extra for seasoning

2 garlic cloves, sliced or finely chopped

1 teaspoon rosemary, finely chopped

360 ml/1½ cups white wine

360 ml/1½ cups water

1 leftover Parmesan cheese rind (optional)

1 potato, halved

200 g/6½ oz. linguine or bucatini

70 g/2½ oz. pecorino cheese, grated, plus extra to serve

1 teaspoon freshly grated nutmeg

Serves 2

Sauté the guanciale, bacon or lardons in the olive oil until the fat flows out. Add the onion and cook for 10 minutes over medium heat until translucent.

Dust the chunks of pig cheek in flour and a few grindings of black pepper. Turn the heat up under the pan, add the cheeks and cook until browned. Add the garlic, rosemary, white wine and Parmesan rind, if you have it. When the wine comes to the boil, turn the heat down to medium and cook, uncovered, for 1 hour.

After 1 hour, top up with an additional 360 ml/1½ cups water if it is sticking on the bottom of the pan, put the lid on and cook for another 45 minutes.

Bring a pan of salted water to the boil with the potato. The starch in the potato will help boost the starch of the pasta water. Cook the pasta until al dente, remove the potato, then strain the pasta, reserving 250 ml/1 cup of the cooking water.

Remove the Parmesan rind and any pieces of fat or gristle that haven't broken down. Use 2 forks to shred the rest of the cheek meat.

Add the pecorino and black pepper to the ragu. Add the cooked pasta and just enough pasta water to bind together into a sauce. Top the pasta with fresh grated nutmeg and a little extra cheese.

Asparagus & Salmon Frittata

This is a wonderful dish for a May day, when asparagus comes into season.

200 g/7 oz. trimmed asparagus

6 large eggs

2 tablespoons cream cheese

finely grated zest and freshly squeezed juice of 1 lemon

150 g/5½ oz. hot smoked salmon, broken into bite-sized chunks

a handful of chopped fresh dill (or parsley, if you prefer)

2 shallots, diced

olive oil, for frying

sea salt and ground black pepper

a 23-cm/9-inch ovenproof frying pan

Serves 2

Bring a pan of salted water to the boil and blanch the asparagus for about 1½–2 minutes. Drain, then immediately plunge the asparagus into iced water to refresh. Drain again.

In a large mixing bowl, combine the eggs, cream cheese, lemon zest and juice, salt and black pepper. Stir in the salmon, most of the herbs, and the blanched asparagus.

Preheat a grill/broiler to high.

Heat a little olive oil in a frying pan/skillet set over a medium heat. Add the shallots and sauté until translucent. Pour the frittata mixture over the shallots and make sure the asparagus is evenly distributed and lying flat in the pan. Cook for about 4–5 minutes.

Drizzle a little olive oil over the top of the frittata, then transfer the frying pan/skillet to under the hot grill/broiler and cook for a further 4–5 minutes, until golden on top. Remove from the heat and allow to cool before removing from the pan.

Little Tuscan Pizzas

These tiny pizzas are great for a lunch or supper. If you can't polish off all six between you, save one or two for your lunch the following day.

15 g/½ oz. fresh yeast, 1 tablespoon dried active yeast or 1 sachet fast-action dried yeast

a pinch of sugar

250 ml/1 cup plus 1 tablespoon warm water

350 g/2½ cups plain/all-purpose flour

about 200 ml/¾ cup extra virgin olive oil

½ teaspoon salt

thinly sliced mozzarella, tomatoes, prosciutto, red onion, aubergine/eggplant, potato or courgette/zucchini

a selection of anchovy fillets, capers or stoned black olives

fine cornmeal, to sprinkle

fresh basil, sage or rocket/arugula leaves, to serve

Makes 6

To make the pizza dough, cream the fresh yeast with the sugar in a small bowl, then whisk in the warm water. Leave for 10 minutes until frothy. if using dried yeast, follow the manufacturer's instructions. Sift the flour into a large bowl and make a well in the centre. Pour in the yeast mixture, 1 tablespoon olive oil and the salt. Mix together with a round-bladed knife, then using hands until the dough comes together. Tip out onto a floured surface. With clean, dry hands, knead the dough for 10 minutes until smooth, elastic and quite soft. If it is too soft to handle, knead in a little more flour. Put in a clean oiled bowl, cover with a damp tea towel and let rise for about 1 hour until doubled in size.

Uncover the dough and knock it back, divide into 6 balls and roll each one into a very thin circle. Put on a couple of baking sheets sprinkled with fine cornmeal. Toss the sliced vegetables in a little olive oil and arrange sparingly on top of the disks along with your choice of anchovies, capers and olives. Season well and drizzle with more olive oil, then bake in a preheated oven at 230°C (450°F) Gas 8 for 15–20 minutes until golden and crisp. Scatter with herbs, drizzle with olive oil and serve immediately.

Simple Tomato & Basil Risotto

It's hard to beat a simple risotto made with fresh seasonal ingredients. Here summer-ripe tomatoes and sweet, liquoricy basil are stirred into buttery semi-cooked rice.

3 fresh plum tomatoes

1 litre/4 cups vegetable stock

65 ml/¼ cup dry vermouth

2 tablespoons butter

2 tablespoons olive oil

2 garlic cloves, chopped

1 large trimmed leek, sliced

325 g/1½ cups Arborio rice

a large handful of fresh basil leaves, roughly torn

50 g/½ cup finely grated Parmesan cheese

extra virgin olive oil, to drizzle

Serves 2

Cut the tomatoes in half and squeeze out and discard as many seeds as possible. Finely dice the flesh and set aside.

Put the stock and vermouth in a medium saucepan set over low heat. Put half of the butter and the oil in a heavy-based saucepan and set over medium heat. Add the garlic and leek and cook for 4–5 minutes, until softened. Add the rice and cook for 1 minute, until shiny and glossy.

Add about 65 ml/¼ cup of the hot stock mixture to the rice and stir constantly, until almost all of the liquid has been absorbed. Add another 65 ml/¼ cup to the pan, stirring until almost all the liquid has been absorbed. Continue adding the stock mixture a little at a time and stirring, until all the stock has been used and the rice is just tender.

Stir in the tomatoes, basil, Parmesan and remaining butter until well combined. Drizzle with olive oil and serve immediately.

Turkey Escalopes

This impressive yet simple to prepare dish makes a lovely meal for two. The crisp crumb on the turkey fillet melts in the mouth and the Green Potato Salad with fresh mint and cream cheese makes the perfect light yet tasty accompaniment. Serve with a well-chilled bottle of crisp Sauvignon Blanc for an effortless and stylish meal.

2 turkey fillets

25 g/2 tablespoons plus 2 teaspoons self-raising/self-rising flour

½ teaspoon fine sea salt

½ teaspoon freshly ground black pepper

75 g/¾ cup dried breadcrumbs

a small handful flat leaf parsley, finely chopped

grated zest of ½ lemon

1 egg, beaten with ½ tablespoon cold water

light vegetable oil, for shallow frying

Green potato salad

1 small handful flat leaf parsley leaves

1 small handful mint leaves

1 garlic clove, crushed

90 ml/6 tablespoons extra virgin olive oil

300 g/2¼ cups kipfler or other new potatoes

a handful baby spinach

3 spring onions/scallions, finely diced

1 courgette/zucchini, shaved into thin ribbons

1 tablespoon cream cheese

a baking sheet lined with parchment paper

Serves 2

Preheat the oven to 140°C (275°F) Gas 1.

Put the turkey fillets between 2 pieces of greaseproof paper. Use a rolling pin to pound it to 5 mm/¼ inch thick.

Put the flour, salt and pepper on a plate. Put the breadcrumbs, parsley and lemon zest on another. Put the eggs in a bowl.

Lightly coat the turkey fillets in the flour and shake off any excess. Dip in the egg, then breadcrumbs. Place the escalopes on a plate. Refrigerate for 30 minutes.

To make the herb dressing for the green potato salad, put the parsley, mint, garlic and olive oil in a blender and whizz until blended.

Put the potatoes in a pan of cold, salted water. Bring to the boil and cook for 10 minutes until tender. Drain and cover the pan. Rattle the pan against the lid to move the potatoes around – doing so will help them absorb the dressing. Stir into the spinach, spring onions/scallions and courgettes/zucchini. Add the cream cheese and herb dressing. Stir to combine. Serve hot or warm.

To cook the prepared escalopes, pour 1.5 cm/½ inch oil into a frying pan/skillet. Heat over medium-high heat until the breadcrumbs sizzle when you toss them in. Reduce the heat to medium and put an escalope in the oil. If you like the crust to stick to the meat, cook for 2 minutes, then turn and cook for another minute. If you prefer the crust to puff, then carefully swirl the pan so the hot oil ripples over the top of the escalope. This should help create the steam that will help it puff. Drain the cooked escalope on kitchen paper/paper towels. Keep warm in the oven on the prepared baking sheet and cook the remaining escalopes. Serve with the green potato salad.

Slow-cooked Pork Ribs

You will need a barbecue to finish off these wonderfully sticky ribs.

1.8 kg/2 lbs. pork ribs (in a rack or as separate ribs, but it is easier to serve the meat if you buy separate ribs rather than a rack)

Marinade
300 ml/1¼ cups smoked BBQ sauce
100 ml/scant ½ cup ketchup
1 tablespoon hot English mustard
1 tablespoon grated fresh ginger
1 tablespoon grated or sliced garlic
½ tablespoon cayenne pepper (or more if you like things spicy)
2 tablespoons marmalade, melted with 1 tablespoon boiling water
150 ml/⅔ cup orange juice
3 tablespoons red wine vinegar

Rhubarb pickle
2 sticks rhubarb
2 tablespoons (caster) sugar
1½ teaspoons sea salt

Serves 2

The night before serving, make the marinade in a large sealable container. Mix all the marinade ingredients together except 100 ml/scant ½ cup of the smoked BBQ sauce and the vinegar. Then add the ribs, put the lid on and leave in the fridge overnight.

Preheat the oven to 120°C (250°F) Gas ½ and put the ribs, marinade and the vinegar in a large casserole dish. Cook for 7 hours with the lid on. Every 2 hours or so, move the ribs around to make sure they're all covered. If the amount of fat leaching out puts you off, you can ladle off some of the cooking liquid and put it in a jar in the fridge for 2 hours to chill, then scoop off the fat that's solidified on top and return the liquid to the pan.

Meanwhile, make the pickle. Wash the rhubarb stalks and trim the scraggly ends. Cut the remaining rhubarb into coins. Sprinkle the sugar and the salt over them. Shake so that all the sides are covered. Set aside for 1–2 hours. When the rhubarb is floppy, drain off the liquid and give them a quick rinse in a colander to remove the excess salt and sugar.

An hour before serving, remove the ribs from the cooking liquid, transfer to a platter and cover with foil so they don't dry out. Heat the barbecue. Before grilling, baste the ribs with the remaining BBQ sauce, thinned with a few tablespoons of the cooking liquid. Cook the ribs on the barbecue until the outside has crisped and charred a little.

Serve the ribs with the pickle and a green salad. And wet cloths to wipe sticky hands on.

The New York Deli Sandwich

This traditional New York sandwich has been given many makeovers through the years.

4 slices good rye bread
6 slices pastrami
2 tablespoons sauerkraut
1 pickled gherkin, finely sliced
75 g/2½ oz. Gruyère cheese, sliced
sea salt and ground black pepper

Russian dressing
2 teaspoons mayonnaise
2 teaspoons ketchup
1 teaspoon creamed horseradish
a pinch of mustard powder

Serves 2

Begin by making the Russian dressing. Simply whisk all the ingredients together in a small bowl and set aside until needed.

To build the sandwiches, start by spreading a generous layer of Russian dressing onto 2 slices of the bread. Add 3 slices of pastrami onto each slice, along with a good dollop of sauerkraut and a few slices of gherkin. Drizzle over a little more Russian dressing and top with slices of Gruyère cheese. Season with salt and pepper and then top each stack with another slice of bread. Use cocktail sticks/toothpicks to hold it all in place, but remember to remove them before eating.

Sardines with Campari, Peach & Fennel

This unusual dish uses the bitterness of Campari as a the perfect foil for the sweetness of the fresh peaches and the saltiness of the fish.

6 sardines or 2 mackerel fillets

2 ripe peaches, pitted

2 tablespoons Campari

3 tablespoons olive oil

1 teaspoon sea salt

1 tablespoon peppercorn-sized
    breadcrumbs

a handful of rustic croutons, made by
    toasting a piece of sourdough and
    ripping it into small pieces

1 fennel bulb, cut into thin strips, fennel
    tops reserved

a handful of fresh mint leaves

1 teaspoon freshly ground black pepper

a handful of black olives, pitted

Serves 2

If using sardines, butterfly them: remove the heads, trim the fins and slit the fish open from the belly down to the tail. Open the fish like a book and place, skin-side up, on a board. Press down with your hand along the backbone to flatten it. Turn the fish over and pull out the backbone, cutting off the tail. Finally, pick out any obvious bones left behind.

Finely grate one of the peaches into a bowl and add the Campari. Set half of this mixture aside in another bowl. Marinate the fish in half of the mixture for 20 minutes.

Heat a frying pan/skillet (or barbecue) over high heat. Add 1 tablespoon of the olive oil, the salt and a layer of breadcrumbs. This will help prevent the flesh of the fish sticking. Cook the fish for 4 minutes on one side, until the flesh is opaque. Flip and cook for 2 minutes on the other side. Add the croutons to the pan to toast them further.

Slice the remaining peach into slivers. Mix them with the fennel, croutons, mint leaves and pepper. Whisk the reserved peach-Campari mixture with the remaining olive oil and sprinkle over the fennel salad. Toss to coat. Serve the fish fillets on top of the salad. Garnish with fennel tops and black olives.

Sangria Prawns

Perfect for a summer supper or a weekend lunch, this recipe can easily be doubled up
if it's more than just the two of you to be fed.

700 g/1½ lbs. fresh prawns/shrimp
(or 350 g/¾ lb. shelled prawns/
shrimp)
1 orange
1 teaspoon sugar (optional)
250 ml/1 cup fruity red wine
160 ml/⅔ cup olive oil
zest of ½ lemon
6 garlic cloves (4 thinly sliced, 2 crushed)
½ red chilli, diced
½ small green apple, diced
a handful of fresh mint, roughly chopped
salt and freshly ground black pepper
bread, to serve

Serves 2

Preheat the oven to 200°C (400°F) Gas 6.

Break the heads off the prawns/shrimp and peel off the shell and legs. Keep the tails on for presentation. Slit their backs with a knife and lift out the black vein. Put the cleaned prawns/shrimp in a bowl.

Using a vegetable peeler, make 3 long strips of orange zest (half the orange's zest in total). Put the strips of zest in a saucepan and add the red wine. Heat over high heat until reduced by two-thirds and the wine is syrupy. Taste and if it's too acrid, add the sugar. Put the prawns/shrimp in a baking dish. Pour over the olive oil. Grate in the remaining orange zest and the lemon zest. Add the garlic and chilli.

Cover with foil and cook in the oven for about 15–18 minutes (the larger the prawns/shrimp, the longer they will take to cook). Once cooked, the prawns/shrimp should be pink and firm, but not stiff to the touch. Drizzle the prawns/shrimp with the red wine syrup and top with the diced apple and chopped mint. Season with salt and pepper.

Serve with bread on the side to mop up the garlic/red wine juices.

Mussels, Fennel & Chickpeas in Pink Wine

This dish is a celebration of the south of France with a pleasing sweetness from softened
fennel and shellfish and a nuttiness from the chickpeas.

1 kg/2¼ lbs. mussels
1 tablespoon olive oil
3 garlic cloves, thinly sliced
1 fennel bulb, trimmed and finely diced
1 x 400-g/14-oz. can chickpeas, rinsed
and drained
200 ml/¾ cup dry rosé wine
4 tablespoons chopped fresh flat leaf
parsley
bread, for dipping

Serves 2

Put the mussels in a sink of cold water. Get rid of any that are open and won't close when you tap them against the side of the sink. Remove the hairy tuft of beard from each mussel.

Heat the olive oil in a heavy-based saucepan. Sauté the garlic and fennel over medium heat until translucent. Add the chickpeas and toss to coat them in the olive oil. Add the mussels, wine and half the parsley to the pan. Turn up the heat and clamp on the lid. Steam for 5 minutes until all the mussels have opened (discard any that don't).

Transfer the mussels, chickpeas and broth to 2 bowls. Top with the remaining parsley. Place the bread in the centre of the table, along with an extra bowl for the shells.

Halibut with Fennel, Olives & Tomato

This delicate fish dish is delicious served with the fennel and tomatoes. However, it is now listed as endangered, so it is crucial to buy only sustainably caught halibut. Look for the blue MSC label or ask your fishmonger.

2 fennel bulbs

extra virgin olive oil

sea salt and freshly ground black pepper

½ lemon

125 g/4 oz. plum tomatoes

red wine vinegar

bunch of fresh parsley, finely chopped

1 garlic clove, finely chopped

2 x 150-g/5-oz. halibut fillets, skin on

1 tablespoons black and green olives,
   pitted

Serves 2

Preheat the oven to 200°C (400°F) Gas 6.

Cut the base and tops off the fennel bulbs and remove the tough outer layer. Cut into quarters, then toss with at least 2 tablespoons oil in a bowl until well coated. Season with a pinch of salt and transfer to a baking sheet. Peel the zest off half a lemon in large pieces and add to the fennel. Cover with foil and bake in the preheated oven for about 35 minutes (more for large bulbs), until quite soft. A sharp knife should glide into the middle without any resistance. Remove the foil and roast for a further 10 minutes or until they colour a little bit.

Toss the tomatoes in enough oil to coat them liberally, season well with salt and ½ tablespoon vinegar. Roast them on a separate baking sheet in the oven with the fennel until the skins pop open – about 15 minutes. Time it so that the fennel and tomatoes both finish cooking around the same time. While the vegetables are roasting, combine the parsley and garlic with enough oil – about 2 or 3 tablespoons – to make a thick parsley oil. Add the olives and season with a pinch of salt.

When the vegetables have finished roasting, turn the oven off and let them sit in the residual heat.

Put a saucepan over medium heat and add 1 tablespoon oil. Season the halibut fillets with salt and pepper and drizzle oil over both sides of the fillet. Once the pan is hot, place the halibut fillets the pan, skin side down. Let them sizzle for about 2–3 minutes, then turn over and cook for another 2–3 minutes (depending on the thickness of your fillet) until they are just cooked through.

Serve the fennel with the tomatoes dotted around it. Place a halibut fillet on top, skin side up. Stir the parsley oil and spoon a good amount over the fish, fennel and tomatoes, making sure to get the olives in too. Serve immediately.

Chicken with Yellow Bean Sauce & Rainbow Peppers

Ideal for quick and casual entertaining, this isn't just a routine stir-fry — the distinctive taste of yellow bean sauce and the colourful combination of red and yellow peppers make for a memorable dish.

2 large skinless chicken breasts,
cut into 2.5-cm/1-inch pieces

1 tablespoon peanut oil

1 red (bell) pepper, seeded and
thinly sliced

1 yellow (bell) pepper, seeded and
thinly sliced

2 tablespoons yellow bean sauce

½ tablespoon light soy sauce

70 ml/⅓ cup chicken stock

2 teaspoons cornflour/cornstarch

cooked rice tossed with toasted sesame
oil, to serve

1 tablespoon slivered almonds,
lightly toasted in a frying pan/skillet,
to garnish (optional)

Marinade

½ tablespoon Chinese rice wine
or dry sherry

1 tablespoon light soy sauce

1 teaspoon toasted sesame oil

½ teaspoon sugar

1 teaspoon finely grated fresh ginger

a pinch of dried chilli/red pepper flakes

Serves 2

Combine all the marinade ingredients in a bowl, then add the chicken pieces and mix well. Cover and marinate in the fridge for 10–15 minutes.

Heat the oil in a wok or large frying pan/skillet until hot, then add the chicken and stir-fry over high heat for 3–4 minutes until golden, well sealed, and nearly cooked through. Remove from the wok and set aside.

Add the peppers to the wok and stir-fry over high heat for 2 minutes. Return the chicken to the wok and add the yellow bean sauce. Cook for 1 minute, stirring occasionally.

Meanwhile, combine the soy sauce, stock, and cornflour/cornstarch in a bowl with 2 tablespoons cold water. Stir until smooth, then pour into the wok. Simmer gently until the sauce has thickened and the chicken is cooked through.

Divide between 2 bowls and serve with the oil-tossed rice. Sprinkle with slivered almonds, if using, to garnish.

Soy Salmon, Wasabi Mash & Pak Choi

The heat of wasabi is a wonderful way to liven up regular mashed potatoes, and the flavour goes really well with soy- and sesame-marinated salmon.

3 tablespoons dark soy sauce

toasted sesame oil

1 teaspoon agave syrup

fresh juice of 1 lime

2 salmon fillets

500 g/1 lb. potatoes

100 g/3½ oz. pak choi/bok choy, halved
  lengthways if fat

extra virgin olive oil

100 ml/6 tablespoons soy cream/creamer

1 spring onion/scallion

wasabi paste or powder

1 teaspoon sesame seeds, lightly toasted

sea salt

Serves 2

Mix together the soy sauce, 1 tablespoon sesame oil, the agave syrup and lime juice in a resealable bag. Place the salmon fillets inside, seal the bag and marinate for at least 20 minutes, or for a few hours if you have the time.

Put the potatoes in a saucepan of cold, salted water. Bring to the boil and cook until just tender. While the potatoes are cooking, bring another pan of water to the boil, add salt and cook the pak choi/bok choy for a few minutes until tender. Drain and season with a drizzle of olive oil and a few drops of sesame oil. When the potatoes are cooked, drain and place a dry tea towel on top to absorb any remaining moisture. After a few minutes, peel the potatoes by just pulling off the skin. Add the soy cream/creamer, plenty of olive oil and the spring onion/scallion and mash until smooth. Season with salt, then cautiously add some wasabi paste or powder. It should be strong enough to taste it though.

When the potatoes are mashed, heat a dry pan over medium heat and add the salmon (reserving the marinade). Fry for 3–4 minutes, then flip over and fry until just cooked through. A minute or so before it is done, add the remaining marinade. Let it bubble, then remove from the heat. Plate up the mash, place the salmon and pak choi/bok choy on top. Sprinkle over the sesame seeds.

Pork with Chilli & Thai Sweet Basil

Pork fillet is given a spicy boost with classic Thai flavourings and the toasted coconut finishes off this super-tasty stir-fry perfectly.

2–3 tablespoons grated fresh coconut
  (or desiccated, if necessary)

300 g/10 oz. pork fillet/tenderloins

1 tablespoon vegetable oil

1.5-cm/½-inch piece of fresh ginger

1 garlic clove, thinly sliced

2 whole bird's-eye chillies

½ lemongrass stalk, outer skin removed
  and bottom 3 cm/1 inch bruised

½ tablespoon fish sauce

1 tablespoon chilli sauce

a small handful of Thai sweet basil

sea salt and freshly ground black pepper

cooked rice or noodles, to serve

Serves 2

Heat a wok or large frying pan/skillet until hot. Add the coconut and dry-fry over high heat for a few minutes until golden. Remove from the wok and set aside.

Put the pork fillet between 2 sheets of clingfilm/plastic wrap and hit with a rolling pin until you have flattened it to about 2 cm/1 inch. Slice very thinly and season with sea salt and black pepper.

Heat the oil in a wok or large frying pan/skillet until hot, then sear the pork in 2 or 3 batches over high heat, adding more oil if necessary. Remove the pork from the wok and set aside.

Add the ginger, garlic, chillies and lemongrass to the wok and stir-fry for 1 minute. Return the pork to the wok and stir for 1 minute. Add the fish sauce and chilli sauce and stir well. Cook for 2 minutes, or until the pork is completely cooked through. Remove from the heat and stir in the Thai sweet basil. Divide between 2 bowls and serve immediately with rice or noodles, garnished with the toasted coconut.

Beef Chow Mein

Chow mein is a classic noodle stir-fry that should be part of every keen cook's repertoire. Treat this recipe as a basic guide to which you can add your own touches. Try varying the vegetables and replacing the beef with chicken or even tofu.

300 g/10 oz. sirloin beef or fillet, trimmed of fat and very thinly sliced

300 g/10 oz. fresh medium egg noodles

1½ tablespoons peanut oil

3 spring onions/scallions, finely chopped, white and green parts kept separately

170 g/6 oz. choy sum (or pak choi/bok choy), chopped into 2-cm/1-inch pieces, stalks and leaves kept separately

1 red chilli, thinly sliced, to garnish (optional)

Marinade

1½ tablespoons dark soy sauce

½ tablespoon Chinese rice wine

½ teaspoon sugar

1 garlic clove, crushed

1 teaspoon finely grated fresh ginger

2 teaspoons cornflour/cornstarch

Sauce

2 tablespoons oyster sauce

200 ml/¾ cup chicken stock

1 tablespoon light soy sauce

1 tablespoon dark soy sauce

2 teaspoons cornflour/cornstarch

Serves 2

Put the beef in a bowl, add all the marinade ingredients, mix well and set aside.

Bring a saucepan of water to the boil. Throw in the noodles and blanch for 2–3 minutes. Drain and rinse under cold running water. Set aside.

Combine all the sauce ingredients in a bowl and set aside.

Heat 1 tablespoon of the oil in a wok or large frying pan/skillet until hot. Add the marinated beef in 2 batches and stir-fry over high heat for 2–3 minutes, or until well sealed all over. Remove the beef from the wok and set aside.

Heat the remaining oil in the wok, then add the white parts of the spring onions/scallions and stir-fry for just 30 seconds. Add the stalks of the choy sum and stir-fry for 2 minutes. Pour in the sauce and bring to the boil. Leave to bubble for 1 minute, then return the beef to the wok and stir through.

Stir the drained noodles into the wok, then cook for 1–2 minutes, or until the noodles are tender. Divide the chow mein between 2 bowls, garnish with the remaining spring onions/scallions and the chilli, if using, and serve immediately.

Chickpea & Fresh Spinach Curry

Chickpeas are a great staple and work brilliantly here in this spicy curry.

1 white onion, roughly chopped

1 garlic clove, sliced

1 teaspoon chopped fresh ginger

1 tablespoon light olive oil

1 tablespoon mild curry paste

200 g/7 oz. canned chopped tomatoes

200 g/7 oz. canned chickpeas, well
    drained and rinsed

250 g/8 oz. fresh spinach, stalks
    removed and leaves chopped

a small handful of fresh coriander/cilantro
    leaves, chopped

naan or roti bread, to serve

Serves 2

Put the onion, garlic and ginger in a food processor and process until finely chopped. Heat the oil in a frying pan/skillet set over high heat. Add the onion mixture and cook for 4–5 minutes, stirring often, until golden. Add the curry paste and stir-fry for just 2 minutes, until aromatic.

Stir in the tomatoes, 125 ml/$\frac{1}{2}$ cup cold water and the chickpeas. Bring to the boil, then reduce the heat to a medium simmer and cook, uncovered, for 10 minutes. Stir in the spinach and cook just until it is wilted.

Stir in the coriander/cilantro and serve with the Indian bread of your choice.

Lamb Rogan Josh

This slow-cooked lamb stew is perfect for hassle-free dining as it almost cooks itself!

1 tablespoon sunflower oil

400 g/12 oz. boneless lamb shoulder,
    cut into large bite-sized pieces

1 large onion, thickly sliced

2 garlic cloves, crushed

1 teaspoon finely grated fresh ginger

1 cassia bark or cinnamon stick

1 teaspoon Kashmiri chilli powder

1 teaspoon paprika

3 cardamom pods

2 tablespoons medium curry paste

200 g/7 oz. canned chopped tomatoes

3 tablespoons tomato purée/paste

$\frac{1}{2}$ teaspoon sugar

200 ml/1 scant cup lamb stock

2–3 potatoes, peeled and left whole

freshly chopped coriander/cilantro
    leaves, to garnish

whisked plain yogurt, to drizzle

Serves 2

Heat half the sunflower oil in a large, heavy-based casserole dish and cook the lamb, in batches, for 3–4 minutes, until evenly browned. Remove with a slotted spoon and set aside.

Add the remaining oil to the dish and add the onions. Cook over medium heat for 10–12 minutes, stirring often, until soft and lightly browned.

Add the garlic, ginger, cassia, chilli powder, paprika and cardamom pods. Stir-fry for 1–2 minutes, then add the curry paste and lamb. Stir-fry for 2–3 minutes, then stir in the canned tomatoes, tomato purée/paste, sugar, stock and potatoes. Season well and bring to the boil. Reduce the heat to very low (using a heat diffuser if possible) and cover tightly. Simmer gently for 2–2$\frac{1}{2}$ hours, or until the lamb is meltingly tender.

Remove from the heat and garnish with the coriander/cilantro and a drizzle of yogurt.

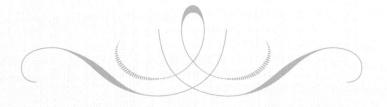

Feeding a Crowd

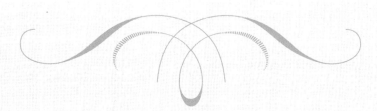

Pasta, Parmesan & Cherry Tomato Pies

This is a take on the classic Scottish macaroni pie or 'peh'. These are delicious served freshly baked out of the oven. This type of pie always has a 1-cm/½-inch rim of pastry extending above the filling to provide a space for adding extra mashed potatoes, baked beans, brown sauce or gravy. These are delicious served freshly baked out of the oven.

1 quantity Rich Hot-water Crust Pastry (see below)

110 g/4 oz. (about 1 cup) dried pasta shapes (such as smaller rigatoni, fusilli, tubetti or macaroni)

40 g/3 tablespoons butter

2½ tablespoons plain/all-purpose flour

a pinch of cayenne pepper

a pinch of English mustard powder

350 ml/1½ cups milk

100 g/1½ cups grated strong Cheddar cheese

30 cherry or baby plum tomatoes, halved

50 g/²⁄₃ cup grated Parmesan cheese

salt and freshly ground black pepper

6 x 10-cm/4-inch straight-sided ramekins, jars, chef's rings or other small pie moulds

Rich hot-water crust pastry

450 g/3²⁄₃ cups plain/all-purpose flour

1 teaspoon salt

2 eggs, beaten

160 g/²⁄₃ cup lard (or half lard, half butter)

100 ml/6 tablespoons water

100 ml/6 tablespoons milk

Makes about 900 g/2 lbs. (enough for two decorated raised pies or 6–8 10-cm/4-inch small pie crusts)

Serves 6

Start making the pie crusts the day before. Follow the recipe below, and while the pastry is chilling, cover the chosen pie moulds with clingfilm/plastic wrap.

Divide the pastry dough into 6 pieces. On a lightly floured surface, roll out each piece thinly, drape over the upturned base of each mould and smooth gently to fit. Don't worry about uneven edges – these will be trimmed off later. Set on a tray and chill or freeze for 30 minutes. When firmly set, use a sharp knife to trim the pastry on each mould to 5 cm/2 inches deep. Carefully ease the pie crusts out of the moulds and pull out the clingfilm/plastic wrap. Set the pie crusts on a tray and leave to dry out in a cool, dry place for 24 hours.

Preheat the oven to 200°C (400°F) Gas 6.

Cook the pasta according to the package instructions. While the pasta is cooking, melt the butter in a medium saucepan and add the flour, cayenne pepper and mustard powder. Cook, stirring, for 1 minute. Remove from the heat. Pour in the milk and whisk in well. Return to the heat and stir until boiling. Simmer, stirring all the time, for 2 minutes.

Drain the pasta well and stir into the sauce. Season to taste and stir in the grated Cheddar. Set aside and leave to cool until tepid.

Spoon the pasta sauce into the dried pie crusts, leaving enough of a rim of pastry projecting above to hold the tomatoes. Pile the tomato halves over the surface of the pies and sprinkle with the Parmesan. Stand the pies in a shallow baking pan and bake in the preheated oven for 10–15 minutes to set the pastry. Reduce the oven temperature to 180°C (350°F) Gas 4 and bake for a further 20 minutes, or until golden and bubbling.

Rich hot-water crust pastry

Sift the flour and salt together into a mixing bowl. Make a well in the centre and pour in the eggs, flicking a little flour over the top.

Put the lard (and butter), milk and water into a saucepan and slowly bring to the boil. Do not let it boil before the fat is melted. Pour the boiling liquid into the flour and mix with a round-bladed knife.

Tip out onto a lightly floured surface and knead lightly until smooth and no longer streaky. Wrap in clingfilm/plastic wrap and chill for at least 30 minutes before rolling out and using in the recipe.

Chicken Pot Pie

This adaptation of a classic recipe is designed to be quick comfort food, so uses crème fraîche rather than a white sauce.

55 g/4 tablespoons butter

1 large leek, trimmed and sliced

2 carrots, peeled and diced

450 g/1 lb. skinless, boneless chicken breast, cubed

about 8 leaves of fresh tarragon, chopped

3 tablespoons chopped fresh flat leaf parsley

150 g/generous 1 cup fresh or frozen peas

250 ml/1 cup crème fraîche or double/heavy cream

1 quantity Rough Puff Pastry (see below)

2 egg yolks, lightly beaten with a pinch of salt, to glaze

salt and freshly ground black pepper

4 x 250-ml/1-cup ovenproof dishes

Rough puff pastry

250 g/2 cups plain/all-purpose flour

a pinch of salt

150 g/10 tablespoons unsalted butter, chilled

about 150 ml/⅔ cup ice-cold water

Makes about 550 g/1¼ lbs. (enough to line or make a 30-cm/12-inch pie plate or base) or 4 individual pie tops

Serves 4

Start by making the pastry – see recipe below.

Melt the butter in a medium saucepan and add the leek and carrots. Cook for about 10 minutes or until they are both soft and cooked through. Add the chicken, stir well and cook for about 10 minutes until the chicken is cooked through. Stir in the tarragon and parsley, followed by the peas and crème fraîche. Bring to the boil, then remove from the heat and set aside.

Roll out the pastry on a lightly floured surface and cut four round discs at least 2.5 cm/ 1 inch wider than the diameter of your ovenproof dishes.

Spoon the chicken filling evenly into the dishes, brush the edges of the dishes with a little beaten egg yolk and top each with a pastry round. Press the pastry firmly down onto the edges of the dishes to seal. You may like to crimp or fork the edges, but keep it fairly casual. (There's need for a hole in the lid of these – the puff pastry wants to rise up into a dome.) Brush with beaten egg yolk and chill for at least 30 minutes.

Preheat the oven to 200°C (400°F) Gas 6. Remove the pies from the fridge, brush with more beaten egg yolk (thinned down with a little water or milk if necessary) to build up a nice glaze, set them on a large baking sheet. Bake in the preheated oven for about 20 minutes or until the pastry tops are puffed and golden brown and the pies are bubbling hot inside.

Rough puff pastry

Sift the flour and salt together into a large mixing bowl. Quickly cut the butter into small cubes, about the size of the top of your little finger. Stir the butter into the flour with a round-bladed knife so that it is evenly distributed. Drizzle the water over the surface, then mix with the knife until the dough starts to come together in a messy lump.

Tip out onto a lightly floured surface and knead lightly until it forms a streaky, rather lumpy ball. Flatten the ball with the palm of your hand and wrap in clingfilm/plastic wrap. Chill for 30 minutes until firm.

Roll the pastry into a long rectangle, three times longer than it is wide (no exact measurements needed here, but it should be about 1 cm/½ inch thick). Mark the pastry lightly into 3 equal sections with a blunt knife. Now fold the third closest to you up over the middle third. Brush off any excess flour with a dry pastry brush, then bring the top third over towards you to cover the folded two thirds.

Give the pastry a quarter turn anti-clockwise so that it looks like a closed book. Seal the edges lightly with a rolling pin to stop them sliding out of shape. Now roll out, always away from you in one direction, until it is the same-sized rectangle as before. Fold in the bottom and top thirds in the same way as before, wrap in clingfilm/plastic wrap and chill for 15 minutes. Do this rolling and folding four more times, then the pastry is ready to use in the recipe.

Salmon, Basil & Parmesan Pasta Bake

Serve this hearty and nutritious recipe with plenty of fresh green vegetables.

a handful of coarse sea salt

500 g/1 lb. pasta tubes of your choice

500 g/1 lb. boneless, skinless salmon
fillets

600 ml/2$\frac{1}{2}$ cups double/heavy cream

leaves from a small bunch of fresh basil,
chopped, reserving a few whole leaves
to serve

200 g/1$\frac{2}{3}$ cups grated medium Cheddar
cheese

100 g/1$\frac{1}{4}$ cups grated Parmesan cheese

50 g/1 cup fresh breadcrumbs

fine sea salt and freshly ground black
pepper

Serves 6–8

Cook the pasta according to the packet instructions. Preheat the oven to 200°C (400°F) Gas 6.

Arrange the salmon fillets in a single layer on a baking sheet and bake until cooked through and the flesh flakes easily. Remove and let cool slightly.

Preheat the grill/broiler to medium-hot.

Put the cream and chopped basil in a saucepan and bring just to the boil, stirring occasionally. Remove from the heat, add the cheeses and stir well to melt.

Flake the salmon and put it in a large bowl. Add the cooked pasta, pour over the hot cream sauce and mix well. Taste and adjust the seasoning. Transfer the pasta to a baking dish and spread evenly. Top with a good grinding of black pepper and sprinkle the breadcrumbs evenly over the top. Grill/broil for 5–10 minutes until the top is crunchy and golden brown. Scatter over the remaining basil leaves and serve immediately.

Truffled Mac 'n' Cheese

For the best results, use high-quality cheeses. Choose a mature/sharp Cheddar,

a Parmesan Reggiano and Lincolnshire Poacher or Gruyère.

a handful of coarse sea salt

500 g/1 lb. macaroni

2 tablespoons truffle paste or truffle oil

1 preserved truffle, finely chopped,
reserving 3 slices to decorate

50 g/1 cup fresh breadcrumbs

fine sea salt and freshly ground black
pepper

Béchamel sauce

50 g/3$\frac{1}{2}$ tablespoons unsalted butter

60 g/6 tablespoons plain/all-purpose flour

625 ml/5 cups semi skimmed milk

1 teaspoon fine sea salt

100 g/$\frac{3}{4}$ cup grated mature/sharp
Cheddar

100 g/$\frac{3}{4}$ cup grated Lincolnshire
Poacher or Gruyère

100 g/1$\frac{1}{4}$ cups Parmesan

Serves 6–8

Cook the macaroni according to the packet instructions. Preheat the grill/broiler to medium–hot.

To make the béchamel sauce, melt the butter in a saucepan. Stir in the flour and cook, stirring constantly, for 1 minute. Pour in the milk in a steady stream, whisking constantly, and continue to whisk for 3–5 minutes until the sauce begins to thicken. Season with fine sea salt. Remove from the heat and add the cheeses and truffle paste or truffle oil, mixing well with a spoon to incorporate. Taste and adjust the seasoning.

Put the cooked macaroni in a large mixing bowl. Stir in the chopped truffle, pour over the hot béchamel sauce and mix well. Taste and adjust the seasoning. Transfer the macaroni mixture to a baking dish and spread evenly. Top with plenty of black pepper and sprinkle the breadcrumbs evenly over the top. Decorate with the reserved truffle slices. Grill/broil for 5–10 minutes until the top is crunchy and golden brown. Serve immediately.

Lamb Kefta Tagine

This Moroccan stew is made in a large pan and is the ideal, fuss-free one-pot dish.

500 g/1 lb. lamb mince

1 onion, grated

2 garlic cloves, finely chopped

a handful of fresh flat leaf parsley leaves,
    finely chopped

2 tablespoons olive oil

1 teaspoon ground cumin

1 teaspoon ground cinnamon

$\frac{1}{2}$ teaspoon cayenne pepper

400-g/14oz. canned chopped tomatoes

a large handful of fresh coriander/cilantro
    leaves, chopped

Serves 4

Put the mince, half of the onion, half of the garlic and the chopped parsley in a bowl. Use your hands to combine and throw the mixture against the side of the bowl several times. Set aside.

Heat the oil in a large heavy-based frying pan/skillet set over high heat and cook the remaining onion and garlic for 5 minutes, until softened and golden. Add the spices and cook, stirring constantly, for 1 minute, until aromatic. Add the tomatoes and 250 ml/1 cup water and bring to the boil. Cook for about 5 minutes.

With slightly wet hands, roll the lamb mixture into walnut-sized balls and put them directly into the sauce mixture as you do so. Reduce the heat, cover and cook for about 15 minutes, until the mince is cooked through. Stir in the coriander/cilantro and keep warm.

Bean & Pork Ragù with Tagliatelle

Broad/fava beans often form the basis of rustic dishes, like this Italian-influenced recipe.

50 g/3 tablespoons butter

1 white onion, chopped

2 garlic cloves, finely chopped

1 carrot, finely chopped

1 celery stick, finely chopped

100 g/4 oz. pancetta, finely chopped

400 g/14 oz. boneless pork shoulder,
    diced

2 teaspoons finely chopped fresh
    oregano leaves

a pinch of freshly ground nutmeg

125 ml/$\frac{1}{2}$ cup white wine

250 ml/1 cup beef stock

400-g/14-oz. can chopped tomatoes

410-g/14-oz. can brown broad/fava
    beans, well drained and rinsed

400 g/14 oz. dried egg tagliatelle

sea salt and freshly ground
    black pepper

freshly grated Parmesan cheese,
    to serve

Serves 4

Melt the butter in a heavy-based casserole set over high heat. Add the onion, garlic, carrot, celery and pancetta and cook for 8–10 minutes, stirring, until the vegetables have softened.

Add the diced pork, oregano and nutmeg and stir-fry for 5 minutes, until the pork is lightly browned all over.

Add the wine and let it sizzle for 2 minutes, until it is almost absorbed. Add the stock, tomatoes and 125 ml/$\frac{1}{2}$ cup cold water and bring to the boil. Reduce the heat to a low simmer, partially cover and cook for 1$\frac{1}{2}$ hours, until the pork is very tender.

Stir in the beans. Using a potato masher, mash the ingredients in the pan, so the pork breaks up and some of the beans are smashed. Season to taste with salt and pepper and cook over low heat while you cook the pasta.

Cook the tagliatelle according to the packet instructions and drain well. Tip the pasta into the ragù and toss well to combine. Serve immediately with plenty of grated Parmesan for sprinkling.

Vegetarian option: Omit the pancetta and pork shoulder and adjust the cooking time accordingly. Keep the quantity of broad/fava beans the same and add a bay leaf and a sprig of fresh thyme for extra flavour. Use vegetable stock in place of the beef stock.

Glorious Golden Fish Pie

This is a real family favourite. The secret of a well-flavoured moist and juicy fish pie is not to overcook the fish and not to pre-cook the prawns/shrimp.

350 g/12 oz. raw shell-on tiger prawns/
shrimp

700 ml/3 cups milk

1 onion, chopped

1 bay leaf

2 peppercorns

450 g/1 lb. fresh sustainable white fish
fillets (such as cod, haddock pollack),
skin on

450 g/1 lb. undyed smoked haddock or
cod fillet, skin on

75 g/5 tablespoons butter

75 g/$^{1}/_{2}$ cup plus 1 tablespoon plain/
all-purpose flour

4 tablespoons chopped fresh flat leaf
parsley

salt and freshly ground black pepper

Saffron and dill mash

1.3 kg/3 lbs. floury potatoes, peeled

a large pinch of saffron threads soaked
in 3 tablespoons hot water

75 g/5 tablespoons butter

250 ml/1 cup milk

3 tablespoons chopped
fresh dill

a 1.5-litre/quart oval pie dish

Serves 4–6

Peel the shells from the prawns/shrimp. Put the shells in a saucepan with the milk, onion, bay leaf and peppercorns. Bring to the boil then lower the heat and simmer for 10 minutes. Turn off the heat and set aside to infuse.

Lay the white and smoked fish fillets, skin side up, in a roasting pan. Strain the infused milk into the pan and simmer on the hob/stovetop for 5–7 minutes until just opaque. Lift the fish fillets out of the milk and transfer to a plate. When the fillets are cool enough to handle, pull off the skin and flake the fish into large pieces, removing any bones as you go. Transfer to a large bowl and add the shelled prawns/shrimp.

Melt the butter in a small saucepan set over medium heat, stir in the flour and gradually add the flavoured milk from the roasting pan. Whisk well and simmer gently for 15 minutes until thick and a little reduced. Taste and season with salt and pepper. Stir in the parsley and pour the sauce over the fish. Carefully mix everything together, then transfer the mixture to the pie dish and leave to cool.

Preheat the oven to 180°C (350°F) Gas 4.

Boil the potatoes in salted water until soft, drain well and mash. Beat in the saffron and its soaking water (if using), butter, milk and dill. When the fish mixture is cold, spoon over the golden mash, piling it up gloriously on top. Bake in the preheated oven for 30–40 minutes or until the potato is golden brown and crispy. Serve immediately.

Chicken & Chorizo with Mashed Squash & Romesco

Romesco is a Spanish, nut-based sauce and a great partner to chicken and chorizo.

8 chicken thighs, skin on and bone in
extra virgin olive oil
180 g/6 oz. chorizo, chopped into chunks
1 red onion, sliced
grated zest of 2 lemons
1 onion/red kuri squash, halved, seeded
    and cut into wedges
a handful of fresh marjoram leaves
sea salt and freshly ground black pepper

Romesco
50 g/$\frac{1}{3}$ cup almonds
30 g/3 tablespoons hazelnuts
16 ripe red plum tomatoes
1 chilli, halved and seeded
4 garlic cloves, peeled
$\frac{1}{2}$ teaspoon sweet smoked paprika
1–2 tablespoons red wine vinegar
4 tablespoons rye or wheat-free
    breadcrumbs, toasted in a little olive
    oil until golden
salt

Serves 8

Preheat the oven to 200°C (400°F) Gas 6.

Coat the chicken thighs in oil, season with salt and pepper, then place in a saucepan over high heat for a few minutes, turning frequently until the skin is sealed and golden brown in colour. Transfer to a baking sheet, skin side up, and add the chorizo, onion and half the lemon zest. Roast in the preheated oven for 45 minutes or until cooked through. If they look like they are beginning to burn, turn the oven temperature down to 180°C (350°F) Gas 4 and leave them in for a little longer, or until the juices run clear when a skewer is inserted.

At the same time, on another baking sheet, toss the onion/red kuri squash with oil until well coated. Season with salt and scatter half the marjoram leaves on top. Bake in the oven for 40 minutes or until completely soft and the skin is beginning to blister.

Meanwhile, for the romesco, roast the almonds and hazelnuts on another baking sheet for 6 minutes or until they go a shade darker. Remove and allow to cool, then place the hazelnuts in a tea towel and rub off the skins.

Toss the tomatoes in oil, season with salt and the chilli and roast in the oven for about 15 minutes or until the tomato skins burst open and the chilli is soft. Using a pestle and mortar, pound the garlic, chilli, nuts and a pinch of salt until you have a chunky paste. Add the tomatoes and pound until all combined together and the skins have broken down a little. Add the paprika and vinegar. Season to taste, then add the breadcrumbs and combine together.

When the squash is cooked through, remove from the oven and place in a bowl. Season with a good pinch of salt, the remaining marjoram (reserving some for serving), the remaining lemon zest and a few glugs of oil. Mash until combined. With something like onion/red kuri squash, it really absorbs flavour and seasoning, so taste it and trust your judgment. If it needs more of anything, throw it in.

When the chicken is cooked, scoop some of the mash onto a plate and nestle the chicken in on top, with some of the juices and chorizo scattered around. Finish with a good tablespoonful of the romesco and the reserved marjoram on top.

Coq au Left-over Red Wine

Start this recipe early as the chicken needs to marinate in the wine overnight.

8 chicken drumsticks

250 ml/1 cup red wine

1 onion, chopped

1 carrot, diced

1 celery stick, diced

4 garlic cloves, sliced

1 dried or fresh bay leaf

4 tablespoons olive oil

12 pickling onions or small shallots

4 bacon rashers, roughly chopped

100 g/4 oz. button mushrooms, stalks
   removed

500 ml/2 cups beef stock

sea salt and freshly ground black pepper

Garlic mash

800 g/2 lbs. floury potatoes, peeled and
   quartered or halved, depending on size

125 ml/¹⁄₂ cup full-fat milk

3 garlic cloves, crushed

75 g butter

Serves 4

Put the chicken drumsticks in a non-reactive dish with the wine, onion, carrot, celery, garlic and bay leaf. Cover and refrigerate overnight, turning occasionally. Set a colander over a large bowl and tip the entire contents of the dish into it. Remove the chicken drumsticks and leave the vegetables in the colander to drain. Reserve the marinade.

Heat 1 tablespoon of the oil in a casserole or large, heavy-based saucepan and cook the pickling onions and bacon for 4–5 minutes, shaking the pan often, until golden. Remove from the pan and set aside. Add another tablespoon of the oil to the pan and cook the mushrooms for 5 minutes, until golden and softened. Remove from the pan and set aside.

Add another tablespoon of oil to the pan and cook half the drumsticks for a few minutes until well browned. Transfer to a plate. Repeat with the remaining oil and drumsticks. Add the drained vegetables, garlic and bay leaf to the pan and cook for 5 minutes, until softened and golden. Return the chicken, pickling onions and bacon to the pan along with the reserved marinade and the beef stock. Bring to the boil, then reduce the heat to medium, cover and cook for about 20 minutes, until the chicken is cooked through and tender. Add the mushrooms and cook for another 5 minutes.

Meanwhile, cook the potatoes in a large saucepan of lightly salted boiling water for 15 minutes, until very tender. Drain well and return to the warm pan. Put the milk, garlic and butter in a small saucepan and cook over low heat until melted. Add the milk mixture to the potatoes and mash or beat until smooth and fluffy. Season to taste.

Rack of Lamb Stuffed with Feta & Mint

This dish takes influences from Persia and adds a hint of Mediterranean to the mix, too.

200 g/7 oz. feta cheese

2 tablespoons finely chopped fresh mint

2 tablespoons finely chopped fresh flat
   leaf parsley

freshly squeezed juice and grated zest of
   1 lemon

2 lamb racks (7–8 cutlets on each rack),
   fat trimmed away to expose the bone
   at each end

3 tablespoons olive oil

sea salt and freshly ground black pepper

toasted pine nuts, to garnish

Serves 6

Preheat the oven to 200°C (400°F) Gas 6.

Put the feta cheese in a mixing bowl and use a fork to mash it until almost smooth. Add the mint, parsley and lemon juice and zest, and stir until combined.

Use a knife to cut down the length of each lamb rack, close to the bones, about 3 cm/ 1¹⁄₄ inches deep, to create a cavity for the stuffing. Divide the feta into 2 and stuff each lamb rack with the mixture. Tie some kitchen twine around every other cutlet to keep the rack together, then place the racks in the prepared baking pan, side by side so they remain upright. Drizzle over the olive oil and season well with salt and pepper. Bake in the preheated oven for 25–30 minutes for medium, or leave 10 minutes longer if you prefer your lamb well done.

Garnish with the toasted pine nuts and serve with couscous.

Seriously Tasty Traditional Texas Chilli

This is a great dish to make a large batch of and then portion and freeze; as with all chillis, the flavour just gets better and better. Serve with rice, a large dollop of sour cream, more hot sauce and a generous handful of grated Cheddar cheese — the perfect dish for feeding a hungry crowd!

1.5 kg/3¼ lbs. best-quality stewing steak (prime boneless beef chuck)

2 tablespoons vegetable oil

3 tablespoons medium-heat chipotle sauce

2 onions, finely chopped

4 large garlic cloves, crushed or finely chopped

3 tablespoons chilli powder

chopped cayenne chillies, preferably Ring of Fire (optional)

2 x 400-g/14-oz. cans chopped tomatoes

750 ml/3 cups hot beef or vegetable stock

140-g/6-oz. can or tube of tomato purée/paste

2 ripe yellow and/or red sweet/bell peppers, deseeded and chopped

1 tablespoon sweet paprika

1 teaspoon dried oregano

400-g/14-oz. can kidney beans

1 teaspoon ground white pepper

3–4 jalapeños, halved lengthways and deseeded

additional hot sauce, to taste

sea salt and freshly ground black pepper

Serves 8–10

Cut the beef into even cubes and remove any sinew; leave a little fat on the meat to melt into the sauce. Heat half the oil in a heavy-based saucepan over high heat, then start to brown the cubes of beef evenly. When this is nearly complete, add the chipotle sauce. Keep the beef moving and coat in the sauce. Remove from the pan and set aside.

In the same pan, gently fry the onions and garlic with 2 tablespoons of the chilli powder and the rest of the oil until translucent. Do not allow to burn! If you wish to increase the chilli heat, add some chopped cayenne chillies and gently soften. Add the canned tomatoes and reheat, stirring occasionally.

Return the beef to the pan with 500 ml/2 cups of the stock and the tomato purée/paste and bring gently to the boil. Reduce to a simmer, then add the sweet/bell peppers, paprika, oregano, kidney beans and white pepper. Stir well and reduce to a very gentle simmer. Add the jalapeños to float on the surface as everything cooks.

Cover and cook over low heat for at least 3 hours, stirring every so often. Add the remaining stock if it starts to look dry. 1–1½ hours before the end of cooking, add the remaining chilli powder and a generous slug of hot sauce, to taste. Season with salt and pepper.

Harissa Roast Chicken with Spiced Vegetables

You can never go wrong with roast chicken, so this recipe, which is a tasty twist on a traditional roast, is a great one to master. This is the perfect dish for a relaxed meal with friends and family: minimum fuss but maximum taste. Any leftovers make a quick supper the following day.

extra virgin olive oil

2 teaspoons cumin seeds

2 teaspoons coriander seeds

1 swede/rutabaga, peeled and chopped into chunks

1 butternut squash, peeled, seeded and chopped into chunks

2 sweet potatoes, chopped into chunks

2 teaspoons ground turmeric

sea salt

2 tablespoons soy yogurt

1 free-range, organic chicken

1 lemon

green salad, to serve

Harissa paste

2 teaspoons each cumin, coriander and caraway seeds

1 red onion, chopped

3 garlic cloves, chopped

2–3 red chillies, seeded

4 jarred Piquillo peppers

3 teaspoons tomato purée/concentrate

2 tablespoons lemon juice

1 teaspoon sweet smoked paprika

Serves 6–8

To make the harissa paste, put the cumin, coriander and caraway seeds in a dry pan and toast for 1–2 minutes until you can smell the aromas wafting up from the pan. Pound to a powder using a pestle and mortar. In the same pan, heat a little oil and very gently fry the onion, garlic and chillies until all soft. Transfer, with the Piquillo peppers, tomato purée/concentrate, lemon juice, paprika, 4 tablespoons oil and a pinch of salt, to a food processor and process until smooth. You may need to adjust the seasoning slightly with a little more salt, paprika or lemon juice.

Preheat the oven to 240°C (475°F) Gas 9.

For the vegetables, toast and grind the cumin and coriander seeds as above. In a bowl, toss the chopped vegetables with 1 teaspoon salt, all the spices and enough oil to coat them generously. Transfer to a roasting pan, making sure to get all the oil and spices out of the bowl and onto the vegetables.

Mix together 3 tablespoons of your harissa paste with the yogurt. Season the chicken with salt and pepper, then spread the harissa mixture all over the skin, pushing some underneath the skin as well. Add some more harissa paste if you want it more spicy. Prick the lemon all over with a sharp knife and place inside the cavity of the chicken.

Place the chicken directly on top of the vegetables and place in the middle of the oven. Immediately turn the heat down to 180°C (350°F) Gas 4 and roast for 30 minutes or until the chicken is beginning to brown.

Remove the roasting pan from the oven, lift the chicken onto a board and stir the vegetables well to make sure they're completely coated in all the juices. Return the chicken to the roasting pan, baste the breast with the juices and continue to roast for a further 40–50 minutes until cooked all the way through; you can check this by inserting a skewer into the leg and if the juices run clear, it is cooked. If the skin looks like it is going to burn at any stage, cover with foil. You do want the skin to be nice and crispy though, so don't cover it in anticipation of burning.

Once the chicken is cooked, wrap the tray in foil for 15 minutes before serving – this allows the flesh to relax and become more tender. Serve with a big green salad.

Slow-Cooked Pork Belly with Soya Beans & Miso

Soya beans can be bland, so add plenty of robust ingredients with distinctive flavours.

100 g/^{2}/$_3$ cup dried soya beans

1 kg/2^1/$_4$ lbs. pork belly, cut into 8 pieces

125 ml/^{1}/$_2$ cup sake (Japanese rice wine)

1 tablespoon peanut oil

2 teaspoons sesame oil

3 garlic cloves, roughly chopped

4 spring onions/scallions, white parts only, chopped

5 thin slices fresh ginger

250 ml/1 cup chicken or vegetable stock

2 tablespoons light soy sauce

2 tablespoons white miso/shinshu (soya bean paste)

1 teaspoon sugar

^{1}/$_2$ teaspoon sea salt

Serves 4

Soak the soya beans in 750 ml/3 cups cold water for at least 10 hours. Drain well and transfer to a large saucepan. Add plenty of boiling water and set the pan over medium heat. Cook for 45–50 minutes, until the beans are tender. Drain and set aside.

Put the pork in a dish and pour over the sake. Cover with clingfilm/plastic wrap and set aside for 1 hour, turning often. Remove the pork from the sake, reserving the sake.

Preheat the oven to 160°C (325°F) Gas 3. Put the peanut oil in a large flameproof casserole and set over high heat. Cook the pork in batches (don't overcrowd the pan), for 4–5 minutes, turning until golden all over. Put the browned pork in a bowl and set aside.

Add the sesame oil to the casserole. Add the garlic, spring onions/scallions and ginger and stir-fry for 1–2 minutes, until softened. Add the reserved sake, letting it boil, and cook until the liquid has reduced by half, stirring to remove any pork stuck to the bottom of the casserole. Add the stock, soy sauce, miso/shinshu, sugar and salt and return the pork to the pan, stirring until the miso/shinshu dissolves. Bring to the boil, cover with a tight-fitting lid, transfer to the preheated oven and cook for 2 hours, turning the pork after 1 hour. Stir in the soya beans, cover and cook for 30 minutes more. Serve hot.

Roasted Pork Loin

Use as much rosemary as you can so the sweet pork flesh in this Italian-style recipe will be suffused with its pungent aroma.

1.75 kg/4 lb. loin of pork on the bone (ask the butcher to bone the loin, but to give you the bones; also ask him to remove the skin and score it to make the crackling)

4 large garlic cloves

4 tablespoons chopped fresh rosemary

a bunch of fresh rosemary sprigs

300 ml/1^1/$_3$ cup dry white wine

extra virgin olive oil, for rubbing and frying

sea salt and freshly ground black pepper

Serves 6

Turn the loin fat side down. Make deep slits all over the meat, especially in the thick part. Make a paste of the garlic, chopped rosemary, at least 1 teaspoon of salt and pepper in a food processor. Push the paste into the slits in the meat and spread the remainder over the surface of the meat. Roll up and tie with fine string, adding some long sprigs of rosemary along its length. Weigh the meat to calculate cooking time – allow 25 minutes for every 500 g/1 pound.

When ready to cook, heat 2 tablespoons olive oil in a frying pan/skillet, unwrap the pork and brown all over. Set in a roasting tin and pour the wine over the pork. Tuck in the remaining rosemary sprigs. Place the bones in another roasting pan convex side up. Rub the pork skin with a little oil and salt. Drape the skin over the pork bones. Place the pan of crackling on the top shelf of a preheated oven, and the pork on the bottom to middle shelf. Roast at 230°C (450°F) Gas 8 for 20 minutes, then reduce the heat to 200°C (400°F) Gas 6 and roast for the remaining calculated time, basting the pork loin every 20 minutes. When cooked, rest the pork in a warm place for 15 minutes, then carve into thick slices.

Fillet of Beef en Croûte

Also known as Beef Wellington, this brings greedy smiles to all assembled around a dinner table. This is real special occasion stuff. Take time to decorate the surface of the pastry lavishly with pastry leaves, flowers or tassels, and remember to give it two coats of salted egg wash with a drying period in between for a rich glossy sheen.

550 g/1¼ lbs ready-made puff pastry,
   defrosted if frozen

1 tablespoon olive oil

1.35-kg/3-lb. piece of beef fillet, trimmed
   of fat and membrane

1 egg plus 1 yolk, beaten, to glaze

Stuffing

55 g/4 tablespoons unsalted butter

2 onions or 6 large banana shallots,
   finely chopped

225 g/8 oz. dark open-cup mushrooms,
   very finely chopped

2 teaspoons chopped fresh thyme

1 teaspoon finely grated orange zest

1 tablespoon balsamic vinegar

100 g/3½ oz. chicken or duck liver pâté

salt and freshly ground black pepper

Serves 6–8

Preheat the oven to 200°C (400°F) Gas 6.

To make the stuffing, melt the butter in a saucepan, add the onions and fry gently for 10 minutes until softened. Stir in the mushrooms and cook, stirring occasionally, for 10 minutes until soft and well-reduced (there should be no liquid left in the pan). Stir in the thyme, orange zest and vinegar, then cook for a further 1–2 minutes. Remove from the heat and beat in the pâté. Season well with salt and pepper and leave to cool completely (this can be made the night before and chilled).

On a lightly floured surface, roll out a third of the pastry to a strip about the size of the piece of fillet. Lift onto a heavy baking sheet, prick all over with a fork and bake in the preheated oven for about 20 minutes until golden brown and crisp. Remove from the oven to a wire rack and leave to cool.

Heat the oil in a frying pan/skillet or roasting pan until hot. Add the fillet and quickly brown all over, turning it often. Remove to a cold baking sheet and leave to cool.

When everything is cold, lay the cooked pastry strip on a baking sheet and place the fillet on top. Spoon the mushroom mixture over the top of the beef (or mould it thinly over the top and sides).

Preheat the oven to 230°C (450°F) Gas 8.

Roll out the remaining pastry to a piece large enough to cover the beef comfortably. Lay the pastry over the beef and neatly wrap it around the fillet, tucking the ends underneath with a fish slice, spatula or palette knife and trimming off any excess. Use the pastry trimmings to make shapes with which to decorate the top.

Brush with the beaten egg, decorate lavishly with the pastry shapes and bake in the preheated oven for 20 minutes. Cover the pastry loosely with kitchen foil to prevent further browning and continue to bake for a further 15 minutes. If the fillet is a thick one, this will cook it to medium rare. If the fillet is from the thin end, give it 25 minutes in total. Allow to rest in a warm place for 10–15 minutes before slicing to serve.

Aubergine & Tomato Gratin

This creamy dish is pure comfort food!

2 red onions, sliced

10 cherry tomatoes – as ripe and red as you can find

extra virgin olive oil

balsamic vinegar

3 aubergines/eggplants, topped, tailed and cut into 1-cm/½-inch slices

a handful of fresh basil leaves

100 ml/6 tablespoons soy cream/creamer

sea salt and freshly ground black pepper

Serves 4–6

Preheat the oven to 200°C (400°F) Gas 6.

Toss the onions and tomatoes with some oil, salt and a drizzle of balsamic vinegar in an ovenproof dish. Roast in the preheated oven for about 15 minutes or until the skins of the tomatoes crack open and the onions are beginning to caramelize. Leave the oven on.

Meanwhile, heat a saucepan over medium heat. Using a pastry brush, coat the aubergine/eggplant slices with oil on both sides. Fry in the hot pan until golden brown on both sides and beginning to soften. Transfer to a dish and generously drizzle with oil. Season well.

Layer the aubergine/eggplant slices in a casserole dish with the tomatoes, onions and basil leaves (reserving some for serving). Pour the cream over, drizzle over some oil and bake in the oven for 15–20 minutes until bubbling and golden on top. Remove from the oven. Tear the remaining basil leaves and scatter over the top of the dish. Serve immediately.

Vegetable & Lentil Moussaka

This satisfying dish makes a change from lasagne and can be made ahead of time.

2 aubergines/eggplants, sliced lengthways

5 tablespoons olive oil

1 red onion, finely chopped

120 ml/½ cup white wine

1 carrot, finely chopped

1 red (bell) pepper, finely chopped

½ courgette/zucchini, finely chopped

a handful of fresh dill, finely chopped

1 teaspoon dried oregano

1 teaspoon ground cinnamon

100 g/½ cup red lentils

400-g/14-oz. can chopped plum tomatoes

600 g/1 lb 5 oz. potatoes, peeled and sliced

400 g/about 2 cups plain yogurt

2 eggs

zest of 1 unwaxed lemon

freshly grated nutmeg

60 g/½ cup crumbled feta cheese

salt and freshly ground black pepper

Serves 4

Preheat the oven to 180 °C (350°F) Gas 4.

Place the aubergine/eggplants on a baking tray, sprinkle with salt and 2 tablespoons olive oil and bake in the preheated oven for 15–20 minutes, until soft and starting to brown.

Meanwhile, put the onion in a large saucepan with 1 tablespoon olive oil and 1 tablespoon water. Cover and cook over low heat for 5–10 minutes until the onion softens without taking on any colour. Take off the lid, add the wine and boil over high heat until the wine has reduced by half. Add the carrot, (bell) pepper, courgette/zucchini, dill, oregano and cinnamon and fry until they turn golden brown. Add the lentils and tomatoes, along with 240 ml/1 cup of water and simmer over low heat for 20 minutes. Season with salt and pepper, to taste.

Fry the potatoes in the remaining 2 tablespoons olive oil until they are golden on either side and the potato has started to soften. Remove from the pan and drain on kitchen paper/paper towels.

To assemble, lay half of the aubergine/eggplant on the bottom of an ovenproof dish, cover with half of the lentil mixture and top with half of the potatoes. Repeat.

To make the topping, whisk the yogurt with the eggs, lemon, nutmeg and half of the feta. Pour on top of the moussaka and sprinkle the top with the remaining crumbled feta. Bake in the oven for 45 minutes until the top is golden brown. Serve hot or at room temperature with a green salad.

Desserts &
Cheese Plates

Rocky Road Cheesecake

This decadent cheesecake is the ultimate chocoholic's indulgence. It has a classic rocky road topping with marshmallows, nuts and cherries, all nestling on a creamy chocolate filling, studded with fudge pieces. This cheesecake is rich so is best served in thin slices!

Crumb case

300 g/10½ oz. Oreo cookies

150 g/11 tablespoons butter, melted

Filling

6 sheets leaf gelatine

320 g/generous 1⅓ cups chocolate cream cheese

250 g/generous 1 cup mascarpone cheese

1 teaspoon vanilla bean paste

100 g/½ cup caster/white sugar

400 ml/1¾ cups double/heavy cream

100 g/3½ oz. mini fudge pieces

Topping

80 g/⅔ cup honey-roasted cashews

100 g/¾ cup glacé/candied cherries, halved

40 g/1 cup mini marshmallows

100 g/3½ oz. chocolate-coated honeycomb balls (such as Maltesers)

100 g/3½ oz. dark chocolate

a 23-cm/9-inch round springform cake pan, greased and lined

Serves 12

To make the crumb case, crush the Oreo cookies to fine crumbs in a food processor or place in a clean plastic bag and bash with a rolling pin. Transfer the crumbs to a mixing bowl and stir in the melted butter. Press the buttery crumbs into the base and sides of the prepared cake pan firmly using the back of a spoon. You need the crumbs to come up about 3–4 cm/1½ inches high on the side of the pan so that they make a case for the filling.

For the filling, soak the gelatine leaves in water until they are soft.

In a large mixing bowl, whisk together the chocolate cream cheese, mascarpone, vanilla and sugar until smooth.

Put the cream in a heatproof bowl set over a pan of simmering water and warm gently. Squeeze the water from the gelatine leaves and stir them into the cream until the gelatine has dissolved. Pass the cream through a sieve/strainer to remove any undissolved gelatine pieces, then add to the cheese mixture. Beat until the mixture is smooth and slightly thick, then stir in the fudge pieces. Pour the mixture over the crumb case and chill in the refrigerator for 3–4 hours or overnight until set.

When set, sprinkle the cashews, cherries, marshmallows and chocolate honeycomb balls over the top of the cheesecake. Melt the dark chocolate in a heatproof bowl set over a pan of simmering water and drizzle it over the rocky road topping. Chill in the refrigerator to set before serving.

Crèmes Brûlées

Crème brûlée is a classic dessert of a rich, creamy vanilla custard topped with crisp caramel. The crème brûlée's origins have long been disputed between France, Spain and England. All three countries have different varieties and all claim to have invented it – France has the brûlée, Spain has crema catalana and England has Trinity cream that was invented in the 1800s in Cambridge.

600 ml/2⅔ cups double/heavy cream
1 vanilla bean, split
6 egg yolks
100 g/½ cup sugar, plus
   2 tablespoons, to dust
1 teaspoon icing/confectioners' sugar

4 large ramekins
kitchen blowtorch (optional)

Makes 4

Preheat the oven to 150°C (300°F) Gas 2.

Put the cream and vanilla bean in a saucepan over low heat and bring to the boil.

Meanwhile, put the egg yolks and sugar in a mixing bowl and whisk with a balloon whisk until light and fluffy. Slowly pour the boiled cream into the egg mixture, whisking vigorously until evenly incorporated. Pass the mixture through a fine sieve/strainer and discard the vanilla bean and any bits of egg shell that may have accidentally crept in!

Divide the custard mixture between the ramekins and place them in a deep roasting pan. Pour water into the pan to reach halfway up the sides of the ramekins. This is called a 'bain marie' and will ensure that the crème brûlées bake evenly and gently.

Bake in the preheated oven for 40–45 minutes. There should still be a slight wobble in the middle of the crème brûlées when you shake them gently.

Remove the crème brûlées from the oven, take them out of the roasting pan and allow to cool completely. You can then refrigerate them until needed, if you like.

When you are ready to serve them, dust the 2 tablespoons sugar over them, followed by the icing/confectioners' sugar. The sugar will give you crunch and the icing/confectioners' sugar will give you shine. You can now blast the tops of the crème brûlées using a kitchen blowtorch, or place them under a hot grill/broiler. When they are ready, they should be a deep orange-brown.

Allow to cool slightly before serving. The caramel will have set and you will have the pleasure of that delicious cracking noise!

Chilled Lemon Soufflés

Soufflés are one of the most iconic French desserts and they can take a long time to master. However, this is a simple lemon mousse made in a ramekin and shaped with the help of some greaseproof paper and an elastic band to make it look like a soufflé.

4 leaves of gelatine

6 eggs, separated

500 ml/2 cups whipping cream

300 g/1½ cups caster/superfine sugar

grated zest and juice of 4 lemons, plus
    extra zest to decorate

icing/confectioners' sugar, to dust

4 large ramekins

Makes 4

Start the recipe the day before you want to serve the soufflés.

First prepare the ramekins. Measure the circumference of the ramekins and add 1 cm/ ½ inch to the figure. Now measure their height and add 5 cm/2 inches to the figure. Take some greaseproof paper and draw 4 rectangles: their length should match that of the recorded circumference; and their height should match that of the recorded height. Cut out the rectangles of paper and wrap each one around a ramekin. Fasten tightly in place with an elastic band or some sticky tape. Place on a baking sheet and set aside.

Put the gelatine in a bowl of cold water to soften.

Put the egg whites in a stand mixer or in a bowl using an electric whisk and whisk until firm peaks form. Refrigerate while you continue with the recipe.

Put the cream in the stand mixer or in a bowl using an electric whisk again and whisk until soft peaks form. Be careful not to over-beat otherwise it will go stiff and grainy and will look split.

Put the egg yolks and sugar in a heatproof bowl over a pan of simmering water (not letting the base of the bowl touch the water). Whisk with a balloon whisk for 5 minutes or until light and foamy. This is called a 'sabayon'.

Put the lemon zest and juice in a saucepan over medium heat and bring to the boil. Remove from the heat and stir in the softened gelatine, squeezed of excess water. Add the lemon mixture to the sabayon, whisking quickly until thoroughly combined. Gently fold the egg whites into the lemon sabayon with a large, metal spoon. When evenly incorporated, fold in the whipped cream in the same way.

Divide the mixture between the ramekins with a spoon – it should reach above the rim of the ramekins by about 3 cm/1¼ inches and be contained by the paper to give you that restaurant 'soufflé' look.

Allow to set in the fridge overnight. The next day, dust with icing/confectioners' sugar and a little extra lemon zest to serve.

Apple & Calvados Croissant Butter Pudding

This is the perfect way to use up stale croissants. The recipe also works really well with Italian panettone at Christmas time.

500 ml/2 cups milk

500 ml/2 cups double/ heavy cream

1 vanilla bean, split

1 cinnamon stick

3 star anise

2 tablespoons Calvados liqueur

3 eggs

3 egg yolks

200 g/1 cup sugar

2 croissants, stale but not too stale

2 tablespoons butter, melted

2 Braeburn apples

2 tablespoons semi-dried apples, chopped

large pie dish or baking pan, well greased

Serves 4–6

Preheat the oven to 200°C (400°F) Gas 6.

Put the milk, cream, vanilla, cinnamon, star anise, vanilla and Calvados in a saucepan over medium heat and bring to the boil.

Put the whole eggs, egg yolks and sugar in a stand mixer or in a mixing bowl using an electric whisk and whisk until pale and fluffy. Slowly pour the boiled cream into the egg mixture, whisking vigorously until evenly incorporated. Pass the mixture through a fine sieve/strainer and discard the vanilla bean, cinnamon stick, star anise and any bits of egg shell that may have accidentally crept in!

Halve the croissants horizontally and brush the melted butter over them. Arrange them in the prepared pie dish or baking pan. Halve, core and roughly chop the fresh apples. Scatter these and the semi-dried apples over the croissants in the pan, then pour the custard in over the top. Using a spatula, press down the croissants so that they start to soak up some of the lovely custard mixture.

Bake in the preheated oven for 25 minutes. It should still be a little runny in the middle. Serve with vanilla ice cream or just some whipped cream.

Vanilla Rice Pudding

This is a traditional English rice pudding which is slow-cooked and develops a lovely golden skin on top. For a variation, add a handful of sultanas/golden raisins.

1 vanilla pod/bean

1 litre/4 cups whole milk

75 g/½ cup golden caster/natural cane sugar

125 ml/½ cup single/light cream

50 g/3½ tablespoons unsalted butter

100 g/½ cup short grain white rice

medium flameproof baking dish

Serves 4

Preheat the oven to 150°C (300°F) Gas 2.

Roll the vanilla pod/bean between the palms of your hand to soften. Split it lengthways with a small sharp knife and use the tip of the knife to scrape the seeds directly into a bowl. Add the milk, sugar and cream and whisk well to combine.

Put the butter in a medium, flameproof baking dish and set over high heat. When the butter is sizzling add the rice and stir for 1–2 minutes, until it is shiny and glossy. Carefully pour the milk mixture into the dish and use a large spoon to gently stir, breaking up any lumps of rice and freeing any grains stuck to the bottom of the dish.

Transfer to the preheated oven and bake, uncovered, for 3 hours, until the top has a golden brown crust. Let cool slightly before serving.

Oaty Apple & Raisin Crumble

A baked fruit crumble, served warm from the oven, has to be one of the most popular comfort puds. And the good news is that compared to most other desserts, it is a healthy choice! Oats add a deliciously crunchy texture to the topping.

2 tablespoons brandy

1 tablespoon runny honey

50 g/⅓ cup raisins (preferably flame)

5 Granny Smith apples, peeled cored and sliced

75 g/½ cup golden caster/natural cane sugar

vanilla ice cream or chilled pouring cream, to serve

Crumble topping

75 g/⅔ cup plain wholemeal/ whole-wheat flour

30 g/¼ cup rolled oats

½ teaspoon baking powder

½ teaspoon ground cinnamon

75 g/2 tablespoons unsalted butter, chilled and cut into cubes

60 g/5 tablespoons light soft brown or demerara sugar

medium baking dish, buttered

Serves 6

Preheat the oven to 200°C (400°F) Gas 6.

Put the brandy, honey and raisins in a small saucepan and set over medium heat. Cook for 5 minutes, stirring constantly, until almost all the liquid has evaporated. Set aside.

Put the apples, sugar and 2 tablespoons cold water in a separate saucepan and set over medium heat. Cover and cook for 10–15 minutes, stirring often, until the apples have softened. Stir in the raisin mixture and let cool. Transfer to the prepared baking dish.

To make the crumble topping, put the flour, oats, baking powder, cinnamon and butter in a bowl. Use your hands to combine all of the ingredients, rubbing the butter between your fingertips, until the mixture resembles coarse sand. Stir in the brown sugar and sprinkle the mixture evenly over the apple mixture in the baking dish.

Bake in the preheated oven for 25–30 minutes, until the topping is crisp and golden. Serve warm with vanilla ice cream or chilled pouring cream, as preferred.

Deep Dish Toffee Apple Pie

In this variation of a classic recipe, smashed-up toffees are added to the apples. As the pie cooks, they melt and cloak the apples in caramel. Cutting through the sugary crust into the golden apples releases a tantalizing toffee-apple aroma. Mixing dessert apples with a proportion of cooking apples sharpens the flavour. Serve with clotted cream or ice cream or, better still, pour cream into the pie through the steam hole just before serving!

75 g/3 oz. hard toffees

1 kg/2¼ lbs. dessert apples (such as Cox's, Russet, McIntosh or Macoun), peeled, cored and thickly sliced

finely grated zest and freshly squeezed juice of 1 small lemon

3 cloves

½ teaspoon mixed/apple pie spice (or cinnamon if you prefer)

1 quantity Basic Shortcrust Pastry (see below)

1 tablespoon each plain/all-purpose flour and caster/granulated sugar, mixed, plus extra caster/granulated sugar for dredging

1 small egg white

23-cm/9-inch pie plate

Serves 6

Basic shortcrust pastry

250 g/2 cups plain/all-purpose flour

a pinch of salt

50 g/3 tablespoons lard (or white cooking fat/shortening), chilled and diced

75 g/5 tablespoons unsalted butter, chilled and diced

2–3 tablespoons ice-cold water

Makes about 400 g/14 oz. (enough to line the base of a 23–25-cm/ 9–10-inch loose-based tart pan or to make a double crust for a 20–23-cm/ 8–9-inch pie plate)

Make the pastry as directed below.

Preheat the oven to 200°C (400°F) Gas 6.

Put the toffees in a plastic bag and use a rolling pin to smash them into small pieces. Add them to a large mixing bowl with the apples, lemon juice and zest, cloves and mixed spice/apple pie spice.

Divide the pastry into 2 pieces and, on a lightly floured surface, roll out each piece to a circle that will easily cover the pie plate. Line the plate with one of the pastry circles and sprinkle the base with the flour and sugar mix. Spoon the apple mixture into the pie plate and mound up in the centre. Brush the pastry edges with a little water and cover the pie dish with the remaining pastry circle, sealing and crimping the edges. Cut off any excess pastry and use the trimmings to cut shapes to decorate the pie, if you have time. Make a slit through the pastry on top to allow the steam to escape while cooking.

Beat the egg white to a loose froth and brush evenly all over the pie, then dredge generously with sugar. Set the pie on a baking sheet and bake in the preheated oven for about 35–40 minutes until golden and firm with a sugary crust.

Basic shortcrust pastry

Sift the flour and salt together into a large mixing bowl. Add the lard and butter and rub in until the mixture resembles breadcrumbs. Add enough of the water to bring the pastry together, and stir in.

Tip onto a lightly floured surface and knead lightly to bring the dough together. Shape into a flattened ball, wrap in clingfilm/plastic wrap and chill for at least 30 minutes before rolling out and using in the recipe.

Tip: To make a vegan variation, simply substitute 125 g/4½ oz. vegan margarine for the lard and butter in the recipe and follow the method as above.

Key Lime Pie

A classic pie from the Florida Keys, where this recipe has been popular since the late 19th century. Some are topped with cream, others meringue. Whichever way you like it, choose juicy fresh limes that are heavy for their size and never make this with bottled lime juice!

Pie crust

200 g/7 oz. mixed ginger nuts and
    digestives/gingersnaps and
    graham crackers
100 g/6½ tablespoons unsalted butter
50 g/¼ cup caster/granulated sugar

Key lime filling

3 large egg yolks, at room temperature
2 teaspoons finely grated lime zest
397-g/14-oz. can sweetened condensed
    milk
150 ml/⅔ cup freshly squeezed lime
    juice (from about 6 limes)
200 ml/¾ cup double/heavy cream
1 tablespoon icing/confectioners' sugar
lime slices, to decorate

23 cm/9-inch tart pan, 2.5 cm/1 inch deep

Serves 8

Preheat the oven to 190°C (375°F) Gas 5.

Put the biscuits/cookies and crackers in a plastic bag and bash with a rolling pin until finely crushed.

Melt the butter in a saucepan, then mix in the biscuit/cookie crumbs and sugar until well coated. Spread the crumb mixture evenly over the base and up the sides of the tart pan, pressing in lightly with the back of a spoon (or a potato masher). Set on a baking sheet with a lip to catch any melting butter that may escape. Bake in the preheated oven for 8–10 minutes, then remove from the oven and let cool. Leave the oven on.

Using an electric hand whisk, beat the egg yolks and lime zest together for about 5 minutes until pale, thick and fluffy. Gradually whisk in the condensed milk and continue to whisk for a further 5 minutes until very thick and fluffy. Now whisk in the lime juice, spoonful by spoonful, keeping the mix nice and fluffy (it will thin down a bit).

Pour the filling into the cooled baked pie crust and set the pan on a baking sheet. Bake in the centre of the oven for about 15 minutes or until just set but still a bit wobbly in the centre. Transfer to a wire rack to cool for 30 minutes, cover and refrigerate for at least 2 hours.

To serve, whip the cream with the icing/confectioners' sugar until thick but spreadable (do not overwhip). Spread or pipe the cream over the top of the pie and decorate with slices of lime. Alternatively, you can just decorate with lime slices and serve with dollops of whipped cream on the side.

Coffee Granita

A granita falls somewhere between a sorbet and a slushy, iced coffee. It's deliciously refreshing in summer – either as a pick-me-up or as a light end to a meal.

4 tablespoons ground coffee
720 ml/3 cups just-boiled water
75 g/⅓ cup (caster) sugar
double/heavy cream, to serve (optional)

large freezerproof container

Serves 1

Put the ground coffee in a cafetière. Pour the hot water over the coffee and let brew for about 5 minutes before pressing down the plunger.

Pour the coffee into the container. (It should be no more than 2–3 cm/1-inch deep.) Sprinkle over the sugar, stir until dissolved, then leave to cool.

Freeze for about 2 hours, or until the coffee starts to freeze around the outside of the container. Use a fork to break up the ice crystals, then freeze for a further 2 hours, breaking up the ice crystals every 30 minutes or so, until you have a thick, icy blend of fine ice crystals similar to snow. Spoon into tall glasses or dishes and serve on its own, or with double cream drizzled over the top.

Peaches & Raspberries in Sparkling Wine

The after-dinner equivalent of a Bellini – and much more enjoyable to linger over on a hot summer's night. Peaches and chilled prosecco are a perfect marriage.

4 perfect ripe peaches
4 tablespoons caster sugar
4 tablespoons raspberry liqueur
  (framboise)
100 g/½ cup fresh raspberries,
  plus extra to serve
1 bottle chilled prosecco wine (750 ml)

Serves 4

Skin and slice the peaches into a bowl, mix with the sugar, liqueur and raspberries. Cover and chill for at least 1 hour.

When ready to serve, spoon the macerated peaches into 4 large glasses. Top up with prosecco at the table, add some extra raspberries and serve with long spoons.

Cheese for Two

We tend to think in terms of large numbers for cheese boards, but cheese is an indulgent treat which will make any cheese lover feel pampered and is an easy-to-prepare part of any dinner. One's instinct when catering for just two people is simply to buy less cheese but while that can be a good strategy with the right cheese, it could seem ungenerous. Rather than putting out big pieces of cheese, cut them into one-portion wedges or slices and put two of each on the board.

• *A generous cheese board for two.* You could have two goats' cheese buttons, two wedges of Camembert or other white-rinded cheese, two slices of Beaufort and two radicchio leaves topped with a spoonful of a soft blue cheese, such as Gorgonzola or Cashel Blue. Perch two pots of fruit compote or chutney alongside, add a few grapes or a couple of fresh figs, some small home-baked rolls or pre-cut slices of raisin bread and some rustic artisanal breadsticks and you've got a very pretty-looking board indeed.

• *A romantic cheese plate for two.* For a more romantic occasion, you could serve the heart-shaped Cœur de Neufchâtel or a truffle-infused cheese, such as Caprini Tartufo. Alternatively, slice a small, deep, round cows' cheese into horizontal slices and sandwich with fine shavings of black truffles, press together, wrap in clingfilm/plastic wrap and leave in the fridge overnight for the flavour of the truffles to infuse the cheese. Serve with rosé Champagne.

• *A summer cheese board for two.* For a summer date, think of partnering cheese and berries: indulge your partner with fine wedges of Chaource, wild strawberries and a glass of pink fizz.

• *A mini-fondue for two.* Sometimes the simplest ideas are the most delicious! You can bake a whole Camembert and it will taste like the most fabulous fondue. Simply take the cheese out of its box and remove the wrapping. Replace the cheese in the box and lightly rub the surface with a cut clove of garlic, pierce the surface of the cheese with a skewer in a few places, then put the lid of the box back on. Bake it in a preheated oven at 200°C (400°F) Gas 6 for about 25 minutes until the cheese is gorgeously gooey. Serve with crusty bread and breadsticks or tiny boiled new potatoes to dunk into the molten filling.

Seasonal Cheese Plates

Ring the changes by serving cheese in a different way according to the season. See below and overleaf for some ideas, but experiment with whatever is in season.

In the Spring
Spring is the time to enjoy the first of the new season's produce, which happily pairs perfectly with the new young cheeses. Decorate your cheese plates with leaves and herbs, accompany them with crisp, fresh white wines, and celebrate the end of winter.

• Serve a grilled/broiled slice of goats' cheese marinated in oil with a herb salad or steamed or charred asparagus. Alternatively, scatter fresh goats' cheese or a white crumbly cheese over a few mixed salad leaves. Perfect with Sauvignon Blanc or an aromatic Belgian wheat beer.

• Serve two contrasting goats' cheeses for comparison – one very young and still soft, the other firmer and more mature with rosemary-flavoured crackers and some herb-marinated olives. Try a crisp rosé this time.

• Do as the Italians do and serve cooked, peeled broad/fava beans, fine slices of Pecorino and shards of Sardinian carta da musica with a glass of Vermentino.

• Another simple but sophisticated Italian idea for an aperitivo: strips of focaccia, Parmesan shavings and a glass of Prosecco.

In the Summer
Take advantage of the wealth of fresh fruit and vegetables to show off your cheeses: fresh berries, watermelon, peaches, apricots, tomatoes and (bell) peppers. Don't be afraid to introduce a touch of spice. Chilli and garlic work well with cheese.

• Serve thinly sliced sheep's cheese with grilled/broiled (bell) peppers and almonds as a mini tapas plate with a glass of fino sherry. Or do as the Basques do and serve it with a cherry compote and a glass of fruity red wine.

• Serve British ploughman's platters with a good chunk of Cheddar, thickly carved ham, a spoonful of chutney, an apple, some crusty bread and traditional English ale.

• Plate up wedges of watermelon, crumbled feta, pumpkin seeds, olive oil and balsamic vinegar.

• Serve a creamy cheese, such as Explorateur, Robiola, or Brillat-Savarin with a peach and a glass of dessert wine.

• Serve a mini antipasto plate with slices of fennel, salami, mozzarella and grilled/broiled artichokes or slow-roasted tomatoes and breadsticks. Drink a light Italian red or white with this.

• A show-stopper: a wedge of Brie, some fresh cherries and a small glass of Guignolet or a Belgian cherry beer.

In the Autumn

*Autumn/fall is the prime time for some of the ingredients that go best with
cheese: apples, pears, grapes, figs and nuts.*

• Serve a wedge of ripe Camembert with sautéed apple slices and a glass of Pommeau.

• A classic but none the worse for it: thin slices of Manchego with membrillo (quince paste) and a palo cortado sherry.

• Try ripe pears, Pecorino, and chilled Poire William: clean and simple.

• Fresh or broiled figs with Gorgonzola and a glass of Maury, a sweet red wine from the Roussillon region of France.

• Give your cheese an Indian twist: try a washed-rind cheese like Munster scattered with roasted cumin seeds, served with mango chutney and strips of warm naan bread. Serve with Gewurztraminer or a hoppy Indian pale ale.

• Two different blues one cow's milk, one sheep's milk with a mixed leaf and walnut salad drizzled with a walnut oil dressing. Surprisingly good with a full-bodied Chardonnay.

• A cheese and jelly plate: Grape jelly and Brie or Sauternes jelly and Stilton.

In the Winter

*Winter cheese plates can take advantage of all the preserved fruits that are available —
luscious big raisins, dates and figs — as well as an array of fortified wines and liqueurs
that come out at this time of year.*

• A Spanish trio of Cabrales (one of the world's best blues), raisins and Pedro Ximénez sherry

• A striking combination: Fourme d'Ambert, toasted walnut bread, poached kumquats and Grand Marnier.

• Two stylish Italian ways of serving Gorgonzola. Drizzle with chestnut honey and serve with griddled panettone and Vin Santo, or serve with a thin wedge of panforte and a glass of Marsala.

• Stilton, oatmeal crackers and sloe or damson gin — a great combination and just as good as port.

• Stilton and barley wine (a strong ale). Strong ales are wonderful with blue cheese.

• Fine slices of Mimolette or Oude Gouda with Medjool dates, dried figs, nuts and tawny port.

• A nibble of good farmstead Cheddar, Brazil nuts and sweet oloroso sherry.

Baking Days

Simple White Bread

This is a basic recipe to start you on your bread-making adventure.

300 g/2⅓ cups white strong/bread flour

6 g/1 teaspoon salt

3 g fresh yeast or 2 g/³⁄₄ teaspoon dried/
   active dry yeast

200 g/200 ml/³⁄₄ cup warm water

*500-g/6 x 4-in. loaf pan, greased with
   vegetable oil*

Makes 1 small loaf

In one (smaller) mixing bowl, mix the flour and salt together and set aside. This is the dry mixture. In another (larger) mixing bowl, weigh out the yeast. Add the water to the yeast. Stir until the yeast has dissolved. This is the wet mixture.

Add the dry mixture to the wet mixture. Mix the mixtures together with a wooden spoon and then your hands until they come together to form a dough. Use a plastic scraper to scrape the side of the bowl clean and make sure all the ingredients are thoroughly mixed. Cover with the bowl that had the dry mixture in it. Let stand for 10 minutes.

After 10 minutes, the dough is ready to be kneaded. Leaving it in the bowl, pull a portion of the dough up from the side and press it into the middle. Turn the bowl slightly and repeat this process with another portion of dough. Repeat another 8 times. The whole process should only take about 10 seconds and the dough should start to resist.

Cover the bowl again and let stand for 10 minutes. Now repeat the kneading/resting process twice. After the second kneading, the dough should resist strongly when you pull it. After the third kneading, the dough should be beautifully smooth. Knead for a fourth time. After the fourth kneading, you should have a smooth ball of dough when you turn it over in the bowl. Now cover the bowl again and let rise for 1 hour. When the dough has doubled in volume, punch it down gently with your fist to release the air.

Lightly dust a clean work surface with flour. Remove the ball of dough from the bowl and place it on the floured work surface. Gently flatten the dough into an oval. Fold the right end of the oval over into the middle. Now fold the left end of the oval over to the middle. Press down slightly to seal the dough together. You will now have a roughly rectangular shape.

Now you can start to shape the dough into a loaf: pull and fold the top of the rectangle one third of the way toward the middle, pressing it into the dough. Swivel the dough 180° and then repeat the pulling and folding. Repeat until you have a neat, reasonably flat loaf shape roughly the size of your loaf pan. Place the dough inside the prepared loaf pan, seam-side down. Cover the loaf pan with the large bowl or a clean plastic bag (blown up) and let rise until slightly less than double the size – about 30–45 minutes.

About 20 minutes before baking, preheat the oven to 240°C (475°F) Gas 9 (fan setting, if possible) or as high as your oven will go. Place a roasting pan at the bottom of the oven to preheat. Fill a cup with water and set aside.

When the dough has finished rising, remove the bowl or covering.

Place the loaf in the preheated oven, pour the reserved cupful of water onto the hot roasting pan to form steam and lower the oven temperature to 200°C (400°F) Gas 6.

Bake for about 35 minutes, or until golden brown. To check if it is baked through, tip it out of the pan and tap the bottom – it should sound hollow. If it is not ready, return to the oven for a few minutes. If it is ready, set it on a wire rack to cool.

Bread Rolls

Bread rolls are a great alternative to sliced bread for sandwiches.

200 g/1½ cups white strong/bread flour

4 g/¾ teaspoon salt

6 g fresh yeast or 3 g/1 teaspoon dried/
active dry yeast

130 g/130 ml/½ cup warm water

baking sheet lined with parchment paper

Makes 4 rolls

Make the Simple White Bread dough on page 145 using the ingredients given here, but following the instructions to the end of paragraph 5. Divide the dough into 4 equal portions using a metal dough scraper or sharp, serrated knife.

Take one portion of dough and roll between your hands until you get a perfectly round, smooth ball. Flatten one side slightly and lay it, flat-side down, on the prepared baking sheet. Repeat with the remaining dough. Cover the rolls with a large bowl. Let rise until slightly less than double the size – about 15–20 minutes.

Meanwhile, preheat the oven to 240°C (475°F) Gas 9 (fan setting, if possible) or as high as your oven will go. Place a roasting pan at the bottom of the oven to preheat. Fill a cup with water and set aside.

When the rolls have finished rising, remove the bowl covering them. Place the rolls in the preheated oven, pour a cupful of water onto the hot roasting pan to form steam and lower the oven temperature to 200°C (400°F) Gas 6. Bake for about 15 minutes, or until golden brown. To check if they are ready, turn one roll over and tap the bottom – it should sound hollow. If not, return to the oven for a few minutes. If they are ready, cool on a wire rack.

Cornbread

This gluten-free bread is great for dipping into stews and mopping up sauces.

200 g/1½ cups fine cornmeal/maize flour

50 g/⅓ cup potato starch

5 g/1 teaspoon salt

5 g fresh yeast or 3 g/1 teaspoon
dried/active dry yeast

200 g/200 ml/¾ cup plus 1 tablespoon
warm water

50 g/½ cup cooked corn kernels (fresh,
frozen or canned and drained)

*16-cm/6½-inch round cake pan, well
greased with vegetable oil*

Makes 1 small bread

In one (smaller) mixing bowl, mix the flour, potato starch and salt together and set aside. This is the dry mixture. In another (larger) mixing bowl, weigh out the yeast. Add the water and stir until the yeast has dissolved. This is the wet mixture.

Add the dry mixture and the corn kernels to the wet mixture. Mix with a wooden spoon. The mixture should have the consistency of soft yogurt. If not, add a little more water to the mixture. Cover and let rest for 1 hour.

Pour the mixture into the prepared cake pan. Cover and let rise until it just reaches the top of the pan – 30–45 minutes. About halfway through the rising, preheat the oven to 240°C (475°F) Gas 9. Place a roasting pan at the bottom of the oven to preheat. Fill a cup with water and set aside.

When the dough has finished rising, remove the bowl or covering. Place the risen bread in the preheated oven. Pour the reserved cupful of water onto the hot roasting pan and lower the temperature to 220°C (425°F) Gas 7.

Bake the cornbread for about 35 minutes, or until golden brown. Let cool in the cake pan and eat warm or cold, cut into wedges.

Olive & Herb Bread

This is a wonderful bread to serve with a platter of cured meats and bowls of olives, either as a snack or a starter course.

40 g/¼ cup green pitted olives or green olives stuffed with pimento

40 g/¼ cup black pitted olives

1 teaspoon mixed dried herbs, eg herbes de Provence

250 g/2 cups white strong/bread flour

4 g/¾ teaspoon salt

3 g fresh yeast or 2 g/¾ teaspoon dried/active dry yeast

180 g/180 ml/¾ cup warm water

baking sheet lined with parchment paper

Makes 1 small loaf

Mix the olives with the herbs and set aside.

In one (smaller) mixing bowl, mix the flour and salt together and set aside. This is the dry mixture.

In another (larger) mixing bowl, weigh out the yeast. Add the water and stir until the yeast has dissolved. This is the wet mixture.

Add the dry mixture to the wet mixture. Mix the mixtures together with a wooden spoon and then your hands until they come together to form a dough. Cover with the bowl that had the dry mixture in it. Let stand for 10 minutes.

After 10 minutes, add the olive mixture to the dough.

Knead gently as in paragraph 3 on page 145 until the olive mixture is thoroughly incorporated. Cover the bowl again and let stand for 10 minutes. Repeat this process twice and let stand for a further 10 minute. Cover the bowl again and let rise for 1 hour

When the dough has doubled in volume, punch it down with your fist to release the air.

Lightly dust a clean work surface with flour. Remove the ball of dough from the bowl and place it on the floured work surface. Gently pull it into a long rectangle. Fold the left-hand third of the rectangle over toward the right. Now fold the right-hand third over. Press down slightly to seal the dough together. You will now have a neat rectangular loaf shape.

Turn the loaf over and place on the prepared baking sheet. Dust with flour. Cover the loaf and let rise until slightly less than double the size – about 30–45 minutes.

About 20 minutes before baking, preheat the oven to 240°C (475°F) Gas 9. Place a roasting pan at the bottom of the oven to preheat. Fill a cup with water and set aside.

When the dough has finished rising, remove the bowl or covering.

Place the loaf in the preheated oven, pour the reserved cupful of water onto the hot roasting pan and lower the oven temperature to 200°C (400°F) Gas 6.

Bake the bread for about 35 minutes, or until golden brown. To check if the bread is baked through, tip it upside down and tap the bottom – it should sound hollow. If it is not ready, return to the oven for a few minutes. If it is ready, set it on a wire rack to cool.

Chocolate Chip Coconut Cookies

Create these heart-shaped cookies for Valentine's Day!

130 g/1 cup gluten-free plain/
   all-purpose flour of choice
60 g/³⁄₄ cup unsweetened
   desiccated coconut
1 teaspoon baking powder
¹⁄₂ teaspoon bicarbonate of soda/
   baking soda
¹⁄₂ teaspoon salt
60 ml/¹⁄₄ cup coconut oil
100 ml/¹⁄₃ cup agave syrup
1 teaspoon vanilla extract
85 g/¹⁄₂ cup dark/bittersweet
   chocolate chips

baking sheet lined with foil
heart-shaped cookie cutter (optional)

Makes 15–16

Preheat the oven to 180°C (350°F) Gas 4.

Mix the flour, coconut, baking powder, bicarbonate of soda/baking soda and salt in a large bowl. You may want to sift the baking powder and bicarbonate of soda/baking soda with the flour first, since it's essential that these are evenly spread throughout your cookie dough.

Make sure the coconut oil is liquid. If it isn't, put it in a saucepan over low heat and allow to melt, then allow to cool completely. Make sure there's exactly 60 ml/¹⁄₄ cup; sometimes it can be a little more or less than the initial quantity. Mix the coconut oil, agave syrup and vanilla extract together. They won't combine very easily because the oil and agave are different consistencies, so give it a good stir. Pour the wet mixture into the bowl of dry ingredients and mix with a wooden spoon. Add the chocolate chips. With your hands, compress the dough into a ball, making sure the chocolate chips are incorporated.

Take 1 generous tablespoon of dough, compress it in your hands and roll it into a ball. You can either flatten the balls slightly on the prepared baking sheet to make round cookies, or you can press the ball of dough into the cookie cutter to mould it into a heart shape. Don't worry if the dough seems a little oily – this is normal. Bake in the preheated oven for about 10–12 minutes, until they start to brown slightly. Remove the baking sheet from the oven and, using a spatula, transfer the cookies to a wire rack and allow to cool.

Gingerbread Men

The gingerbread men are crisp and very moreish when baked.

100 g/6¹⁄₂ tablespoons butter
50 g/¹⁄₄ cup dark muscovado or packed
   dark brown soft sugar
225 g/1³⁄₄ cups plain/all-purpose flour
³⁄₄ teaspoon bicarbonate of soda/
   baking soda
2 teaspoons ground ginger
1 teaspoon ground cinnamon
4 tablespoons golden/corn syrup
1 tablespoon black treacle/blackstrap
   molasses
small coloured sugar-coated chocolate
   drops or halved currants, to decorate

7–8-cm/3-inch (height) gingerbread man
cutter
2 baking sheets, lightly buttered

Makes 18

Heat the butter and sugar together in a small pan until melted, stirring every now and then. Remove the pan from the heat and let cool slightly.

Sift the flour, bicarbonate of soda/baking soda, and ground ginger and cinnamon into the bowl of an electric mixer (or use a large mixing bowl and an electric whisk) and pour the melted butter mixture into it. Add the golden/corn syrup and treacle/molasses and mix to combine. Bring together into a ball, wrap in clingfilm/plastic wrap and refrigerate for 30 minutes.

Preheat the oven to 190°C (375°F) Gas 5. Halve the chilled dough and roll one half out on the lightly floured work surface until it is about 5–6 mm/¹⁄₄ inch thick. Cut out men with the cutter and arrange them on one of the prepared baking sheets. Gently re-form and re-roll the dough, then keep stamping out gingerbread men. Make indentations for eyes and mouths and add sugar-coated chocolate drops or currants for buttons.

Repeat with the other half of the dough. Bake in the preheated oven for 8 minutes, or until they are set and slightly firmer to the touch. Transfer to wire racks to cool.

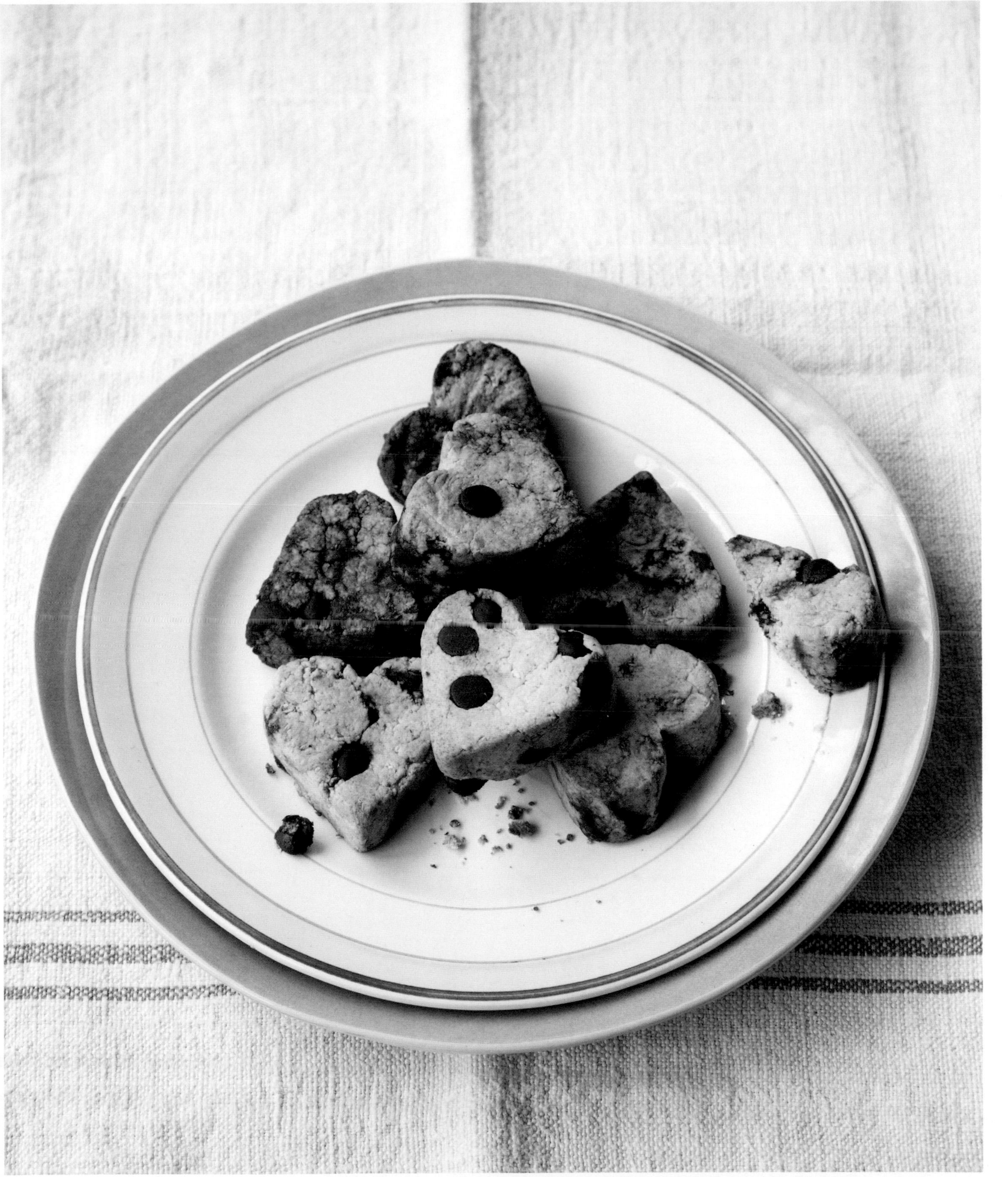

Cherry Marzipan Streusel Squares

These are also a favourite when made with raspberry or plum jam.

100 g/¾ cup plain/all-purpose flour

50 g/3 tablespoons butter, chilled and diced

1 tablespoon icing/confectioner's sugar

5 tablespoons morello cherry jam

Streusel topping

76 g/⅔ cup plain/all-purpose flour

75 g/⅓ cup granulated sugar

25 g/2 tablespoons butter, softened and cubed

50 g/1¾ oz. marzipan, diced

50 g/⅓ cup undyed glacé/candied cherries, chopped

50 g/½ cup flaked/slivered almonds

Almond layer

100 g/6½ tablespoons butter, softened and cubed

75 g/⅓ cup (caster) sugar

2 large eggs, lightly beaten

100 g/ ground almonds

25 g/3 tablespoons plain/all-purpose flour

18-cm/7-inch square pan, ideally loose-based, oiled

Makes 12

For the pastry, put the flour, butter and sugar in an electric mixer and whizz until the mixture resembles breadcrumbs. Add 2 tablespoons cold water and whizz again. Add a few more drops of water, if needed, to bring together into a dough.

Tip the pastry out on a lightly floured work surface and roll out until it is about 3–4 mm/⅛ inch thick. Trim the edges with a sharp knife to make a 19-cm/7½-inch square. Line the base of the pan with the pastry – it will come slightly up the inside of the tin all the way round. Refrigerate for 30 minutes.

Preheat the oven to 200°C (400°F) Gas 6.

To make the streusel topping, tip the flour and sugar into the electric mixer (or use a mixing bowl and an electric whisk) and whizz together. Add the butter and whizz until the mixture is crumbly. Tip into a bowl, if necessary, and stir in the marzipan, glacé/candied cherries and flaked/slivered almonds.

To make the almond layer, mix all the ingredients together in the electric mixer until amalgamated.

Spread the cherry jam on top of the chilled pastry base. Spoon blobs of the almond mixture on top of the jam and spread them out with a spatula. Scatter the streusel topping over the top. Put the tin on a baking sheet and bake in the preheated oven for 40 minutes, or until lightly golden. Cover with foil towards the end of cooking to prevent over-browning. Let cool in the pan before cutting into 12 squares.

Coffee Blondies

Use a vegetable peeler to make piles of white and dark chocolate shavings for decorating these cappuccino-like squares.

100 g/1 cup shelled pecans

200 g/1 cup light muscovado/light brown sugar

175 g/1½ sticks butter

3 tablespoons instant coffee granules

2 eggs, lightly beaten

250 g/2 cups plain/all-purpose flour

2 teaspoons baking powder

a pinch of salt

100 g/⅔ cup dark/bittersweet chocolate chips

To decorate

200 ml/¾ cup double/heavy cream

2 tablespoons icing/confectioners' sugar

mixed chocolate shavings

chocolate-coated coffee beans

20 x 30-cm/8 x 12-inch baking pan, greased and lined with greased baking parchment

Makes 16–20 portions

Preheat the oven to 170°C (325°F) Gas 3.

Tip the pecans onto a baking sheet and lightly toast in the preheated oven for 5 minutes. Roughly chop and leave to cool. Leave the oven on for the brownies.

Tip the muscovado/brown sugar and butter into a medium saucepan over low–medium heat and melt, stirring constantly. In a small bowl, dissolve the coffee granules in 1½ tablespoons boiling water. Stir two-thirds into the pan (reserve the rest for the frosting). Remove from the heat, transfer the mixture to a bowl and leave to cool completely.

Stir the eggs into the pan until smooth. Sift the flour, baking powder and salt into the pan and fold in until well mixed, then stir in the chocolate chips and pecans. Pour the mixture into the prepared baking pan, spread level and bake on the middle shelf of the preheated oven for about 25 minutes, or until just set in the middle and the top has formed a light crust. Remove from the oven and leave to cool completely in the pan.

To decorate, whip the cream with the reserved coffee and sugar. Remove the brownies from the pan, cut into portions, top with a dollop of coffee cream and scatter chocolate shavings and coffee beans over the top.

Blueberry Lime Friands

If you haven't come across friands before, you will soon be converted. Based on the French financier, they are small, light-textured cakes.

125 g/1 stick butter
75 g/½ cup shelled, blanched hazelnuts
125 g/¾ cup icing/ confectioners' sugar
100 g/¾ cup plain/all-purpose flour
finely grated zest of 2 limes
175 g/1⅔ cups blueberries
4 large egg whites

Lime syrup
freshly squeezed juice of 1 small lime
40 g/3 tablespoons (caster) sugar

9-hole friand or muffin pan, well buttered

Makes 9

Preheat the oven to 200°C (400°F) Gas 6. Melt the butter in a pan and let cool slightly.

Whiz the hazelnuts in a blender until finely ground. Sift the icing/confectioners' sugar and flour into a large mixing bowl. Stir in the ground hazelnuts, lime zest and blueberries.

Put the egg whites in a large, scrupulously clean bowl and whisk until they form soft peaks. Using a large metal spoon, gently fold half the egg whites into the flour mixture with half the melted butter. Fold in the other half of the egg whites and melted butter. Divide the mixture between the holes of the prepared pan. Bake in the preheated oven for 20 minutes.

To make the syrup, heat the lime juice and sugar together in a small pan, stirring, until the sugar has dissolved. Let the cooked friands cool for 5 minutes, then make a few holes in the top of each using the point of a small, sharp knife. Drizzle a little of the lime syrup over each of the warm cakes, allowing it to seep into the holes. Leave the friands in the pan until completely cold, before running a knife around the edges and turning them out.

Chocolate Chip Cookies

This recipe differs from a standard cookie recipe as it is vegan (but just as delicious!).

125 ml/½ cup almond milk
2 tablespoons ground flaxseeds/
   linseeds
285 g/2 cups spelt flour
75 g/⅔ cup unsweetened
   cocoa powder (preferably raw)
1¼ teaspoons bicarbonate of/baking
   soda
125 ml/½ cup sunflower oil
190 g/1 cup granulated sweetener
   of choice
1 tablespoon vanilla extract
175 g/1 cup dark/bittersweet
   chocolate chips

2 baking sheets lined with foil

Makes about 16

Preheat the oven to 180°C (350°F) Gas 4.

Mix together the almond milk and ground flaxseeds/linseeds and set aside to thicken for a few minutes. Separately, whisk together the flour, cocoa powder and bicarbonate of/ baking soda in a large bowl.

Add the sunflower oil, sweetener and vanilla extract to the milk-seed mixture and stir thoroughly. After about 5 minutes you'll start to see it thicken up even more.

Pour the liquid mixture into the bowl of dry ingredients and stir to combine. It will look far too liquidy to resemble regular cookie dough, so set it aside for about 10–15 minutes and you'll see it change. Stir it again once thick.

Pinch off pieces of dough a little smaller than a golf ball and roll into balls between your hands. Flatten to discs about 1 cm/½ inch thick and arrange on the prepared baking sheets. They will spread a lot during baking, so leave plenty of space between them. Bake in the preheated oven for about 7 minutes, after which they will seem too soft to remove, but they will harden as they cool. Gently transfer the cookies to a wire rack to cool completely. They will remain gooey and soft in the middle.

Passion Fruit Butterfly Cakes

These pretty cakes look like a summer swarm of fluttering butterflies on a plate.

3 passion fruit

115 g/1 stick unsalted butter, at room
temperature

115 g/½ cup caster/granulated sugar

2 eggs

115 g self-raising/rising flour

1 teaspoon baking powder

To decorate

6 passion fruit

150 g/⅔ cup mascarpone

4 tablespoons icing/confectioner's sugar,
sifted, plus extra to dust

*12-hole cupcake pan, lined with paper
cases/liners*

Makes 12

Preheat the oven to 180°C (350°F) Gas 4.

Halve the passion fruit and scoop the flesh into a sieve set over a bowl. Press with the back of a teaspoon to extract the juice. Beat the butter and sugar together in a bowl until pale and fluffy, then beat in the eggs, one at a time. Sift the flour and baking powder into the mixture and fold in. Stir in the passion fruit juice.

Spoon the mixture into the paper cases/liners, then bake in the preheated oven for about 17 minutes until risen and golden and a skewer inserted in the centre comes out clean. Transfer to a wire rack to cool.

To decorate, halve the passion fruit and scoop the flesh into a sieve set over a bowl. Press with the back of a teaspoon to extract the juice, then add the mascarpone and sugar to the bowl. Mix until smooth and creamy. Cover and refrigerate for about 30 minutes to thicken up. Slice the top off each cake, then cut each top in half. Spoon a generous dollop of the mascarpone mixture onto each cake, then top with the two halves, setting them at an angle to resemble wings. Dust with icing/confectioner's sugar and serve.

Rosewater Cupcakes

Scented with rosewater, these gorgeous pink cupcakes are perfect for a teatime treat.

115 g/1 stick unsalted butter,
at room temperature

115 g/½ cup caster/granulated sugar

2 eggs

115 g/1 cup self-raising/rising flour

1 tablespoon rosewater

To decorate

12 pink rose petals

1 egg white, beaten

1 tablespoon caster/superfine sugar

1½–2 tablespoons freshly squeezed
lemon juice

145 g/1¼ cups icing/confectioner's
sugar, sifted

pink food colouring

*12-hole cupcake pan, lined with paper
cases/liners*

Makes 12

Preheat the oven to 180°C (350°F) Gas 4.

Beat the butter and sugar together in a bowl until pale and fluffy, then beat in the eggs, one at a time. Sift the flour into the mixture and fold in, then stir in the rosewater.

Spoon the mixture into the paper cases/liners and bake in the preheated oven for about 17 minutes until risen and golden and a skewer inserted in the centre comes out clean. Transfer to a wire rack to cool.

To decorate, brush each rose petal with egg white, then sprinkle with the caster/superfine sugar and let dry for about 1 hour.

Put 1½ tablespoons lemon juice in a bowl, then sift the icing/confectioner's sugar into the bowl and stir until smooth. Add a little more lemon juice as required to make a smooth, spoonable icing. Add one or two drops of food colouring to achieve a pale pink icing, then spread over the cakes. Top each one with a sugared rose petal. Leave to set before serving.

Victoria Sandwich with Fresh Mint & Strawberries

The sponges for this classic cake are best eaten as fresh as possible. They are also delicious sandwiched together with good-quality raspberry jam or a citrus curd and some whipped cream.

200 g/14 tablespoons unsalted butter, softened

200 g/1 cup (caster) sugar

4 large eggs, lightly beaten

1 teaspoon vanilla extract

200 g/1²⁄₃ cups self-raising/rising flour, sifted

2 teaspoons baking powder

a pinch of salt

icing/confectioners' sugar, for dusting

Filling

250 g/1 pint ripe strawberries

2 tablespoons icing/confectioners' sugar

grated zest of 1 unwaxed lemon

150 g/²⁄₃ cup crème fraîche or double/heavy cream, chilled

100 g/¹⁄₃ cup mascarpone, chilled

1 tablespoon shredded mint leaves

two 20-cm/8-inch round cake pans, lightly buttered and baselined with baking parchment

Makes 16

Preheat the oven to 180°C (350°F) Gas 4.

Put the butter and sugar in an electric mixer (or use a large mixing bowl and an electric whisk) and beat for 3–4 minutes, or until pale and fluffy. Gradually add the beaten eggs with the beaters still running, followed by the vanilla extract, flour, baking powder and salt. Mix until all the ingredients are combined.

Divide the mixture between the prepared tins and spread it evenly with a spatula. Bake in the preheated oven for 25 minutes, or until lightly golden and risen. Leave to cool in the tins for 30 minutes. Tip the cakes out onto a wire rack and peel off the base papers. Leave to cool completely.

To make the filling, hull and thinly slice the strawberries, then mix in a bowl with half the icing/confectioners' sugar and all the lemon zest. Leave to macerate for up to 30 minutes.

In another bowl, use a balloon whisk to whisk the crème fraîche and mascarpone together until smooth. Stir in the rest of the icing/confectioners' sugar and the shredded mint.

To assemble, place one cake on a board or large serving plate and spread the creamy filling over the top. Scatter the strawberries over the filling. Place the other cake on top and dust with icing/confectioners' sugar.

Moroccan Orange Cake

Naturally wheat free (it is made with ground almonds) and supremely moist, drowned in a sweet orange syrup, this exotic and fragrant cake never fails to impress.
Serve at teatime or as a dessert.

300 g/1½ cups ground almonds

250 g/1⅓ cups xylitol

2 teaspoons baking powder

5 eggs

200 ml/¾ cup plus 1 tablespoon
    sunflower oil

2 teaspoons agave syrup for the cake,
    plus 60 ml/5 tablespoons for the syrup

grated zest and juice of 1 large orange

grated zest and juice of ½ lemon

3 cloves

3 cinnamon sticks

soy yogurt with some ground cinnamon
    stirred though, to serve

*20-cm/8-inch springform pan, baselined
    with parchment paper*

Serves 10–12

Preheat the oven to 180°C (350°F) Gas 4.

In a bowl, mix together the ground almonds, xylitol and baking powder. In a separate bowl, whisk together the eggs, sunflower oil, the 2 teaspoons of agave syrup and the orange and lemon zest. Pour the mixture into the dry ingredients and combine together.

Pour the cake mixture into the prepared baking pan and bake in the preheated oven for 35–45 minutes until a skewer inserted in the middle comes out clean. If the top looks like it is going to burn, cover with foil, being careful not to press on the cake. Allow to cool slightly while you make a syrup.

Put the orange and lemon juices, the 60 ml/5 tablespoons agave syrup, cloves and cinnamon in a saucepan. Bring to the boil, reduce the heat and simmer for 5 minutes.

While the cake is still warm, turn it out onto a plate, drizzle the syrup over and allow it to seep in. If it is not all absorbed at once, keep it aside to drizzle over later. When you are ready to serve, pile the cinnamon sticks and cloves on top of one another on the cake. Serve with the cinnamon-soy yogurt dolloped onto each slice.

Red Velvet Layer Cake

This is a variation on a much-loved classic, with the deep, red cake layers filled and covered in a cream cheese frosting. There's no need for a wildly creative streak or even a steady hand for the chocolate squiggles – in fact, the more swirly and free-style the better!

350 g/2⅔ cups plain/all-purpose flour

3 teaspoons baking powder

1 teaspoon bicarbonate of/baking soda

2 big tablespoons cocoa powder

a pinch of salt

225 g/2 sticks butter, soft

350 g/1¾ cups (caster) sugar

4 large eggs

1 teaspoon vanilla extract

1 teaspoon red food colouring paste
(Ruby or Christmas Red)

250 ml/1 cup buttermilk, room
temperature

To decorate

200 g/6½ oz. dark/bittersweet or
semisweet chocolate, finely chopped

Cream cheese frosting

450 g/2 cups cream cheese

75 g/5½ tablespoons butter, soft

4½ tablespoons clear honey or maple
syrup

1½ teaspoons vanilla extract or the
seeds from ½ a vanilla pod/bean

*three 20-cm/8-inch round cake pans,
greased and baselined with greased
baking parchment*

disposable piping bag

*2 baking sheets, lined with nonstick baking
parchment*

Serves 10

Preheat the oven to 180°C (350°F) Gas 4.

Sift together the flour, baking powder, cocoa powder, bicarbonate of soda/baking soda and salt and set aside. Cream the butter and sugar in the bowl of a stand mixer until light and fluffy – at least 3–4 minutes. Lightly beat the eggs and vanilla together. Gradually add the egg mixture to the creamed butter in 4 or 5 additions, mixing well between each addition and scraping down the bowl from time to time with a rubber spatula. Whisk the food colouring paste into the buttermilk. Add the sifted dry ingredients to the bowl of the stand mixer, alternately with the coloured buttermilk. Mix until smooth.

Divide the mixture evenly between the prepared pans and spread level with a palette knife. Bake the cakes on the middle shelf of the preheated oven for about 20–25 minutes or until a skewer inserted into the middle comes out clean. Let cool in the pans for 3–4 minutes, then turn out onto a wire rack to cool completely.

To make the dark chocolate squiggles, melt the chocolate in a heatproof bowl set over a pan of barely simmering water. Do not let the base of the bowl touch the water. Stir until smooth, then let cool slightly.

Spoon the melted chocolate into the piping bag and snip the end to a fine point. Pipe elaborate swirls and squiggles over the baking parchment. Refrigerate until completely set and firm.

When you are ready to assemble the cake, place one of the cake layers on a serving dish and spread about 3 tablespoons of the Cream Cheese Frosting over it. Carefully place a second cake layer on top and spread another 3 tablespoons of frosting over it. Finally, top with the last cake layer and gently press the cake layers together.

Spread the remaining frosting over the top and side of the cake using a palette knife.

Remove the chocolate squiggles from the fridge and, using a palette knife, carefully lift them off the paper. Gently press into the frosting around the side of the cake.

Holiday
Celebrations

Roast Turkey with Lemon & Herb Stuffing

If this is your first time hosting Christmas, plan everything well in advance and give yourself a generous 40 minutes at the end of the cooking time for the turkey to keep warm and rest, while everything else is finished. See pages 170 and 177 for suggested accompaniments.

1 turkey, with giblets
1 onion, coarsely chopped
a sprig of thyme
1 bay leaf
125 g/1 stick salted butter
sea salt and freshly ground black pepper
Lemon and Herb Stuffing (page 170)

To serve
Bacon Rolls (page 177)
Bread Sauce (page 170)
Sprouts and pancetta (page 177)

squares of muslin/cheesecloth, paper or kitchen foil (enough to cover the breast and drumsticks)

For sizes, serving quantities and cooking times, see the chart on page 204

To make a stock, the day before, put the giblets, minus the liver, but with the neck chopped in half, in a saucepan. Add the onion, thyme and bay leaf. Cover with water and bring slowly to the boil, removing any foam as it rises. Simmer for 2 hours and strain. Taste and, if necessary, reduce to strengthen the flavour.

Make the stuffing (see page 170). Wipe out the neck area and cavity of the turkey with a damp cloth and lightly season the inside. Spoon in the stuffing, allowing plenty of room for each one to expand. This is especially true for the neck stuffing.

Preheat the oven to 180°C (350°F) Gas 4.

Put half the butter in a saucepan and melt gently. Using your hands, spread the remaining butter all over the skin. Soak the muslin/cheesecloth or paper in the melted butter and drape over the bird, with a double layer covering the drumsticks.

Put the bird in a large roasting pan in the middle of the oven. Roast for the calculated time according to size (page 204) except that the oven temperature must be raised to 230°C (450°F) Gas 8 and the coverings removed for the last 30 minutes to crisp the skin. Turn off the oven but leave the turkey in the oven. If you don't have a second oven, leave it on, remove the turkey from the oven, cover with a tent of foil and leave in a warm place.

If you wish, spoon some of the turkey fat from the roasting tin into a second tin and use for roasting potatoes.

Using oven gloves, or rubber gloves specially reserved for the occasion, tip out any free juices from the cavity, then lift the turkey onto the serving platter. Return it to the oven, leaving the door open until the temperature has dropped and will no longer cook the bird. Pour off the gravy juices, preferably into a gravy separator or jug to lift off the fat. Reheat with the seasoned stock. Use to fill a gravy boat, reserving the rest in a Thermos for second helpings. Serve with all your favourite accompaniments.

Turkey Accompaniments

These are some of the classic accompaniments for roast turkey, but also take a look at page 177 for more suggestions.

Wine gravy

4 tablespoons fat from the pan

8 tablespoons red wine

2 tablespoon plain/all-purpose flour

1 litre/4 cups and 3 tablespoons
　well-flavoured stock or water

sea salt and freshly ground black pepper

Serves 8–10

Bread sauce

½ onion, finely chopped

½ teaspoon dried thyme

3 whole cloves

500 ml/2 cups and 2 tablespoons milk

100 g/1¾–2 cups fresh white breadcrumbs

75 g/5⅓ tablespoons unsalted butter
　(optional)

2 tablespoons double/heavy cream
　(optional)

sea salt and freshly ground black pepper

Serves 8–10

Cranberry relish

100 g/1 heaped cup fresh cranberries

100 ml/⅓ cup plus 1 tablespoon cider
　vinegar

3 cm/1¼ inches fresh ginger, grated

½ cinnamon stick

2 juniper berries, crushed

2 cloves

50 g/¼ cup demerara/turbinado sugar

Makes about 250 ml/1 heaping cup

Lemon & herb stuffing

2 eggs

125 g/9 tablespoons butter, melted

a handful of fresh parsley leaves

1 teaspoon fresh lemon thyme

freshly grated zest and juice of
　1 unwaxed lemon

225 g/4 cups fresh white breadcrumbs

sea salt and freshly ground black pepper

Sufficient for a large chicken/turkey

Wine gravy

Put the roasting pan on top of the stove, heat the reserved 2 tablespoons fat, add the wine and reduce to 3 tablespoons. Add the flour, stir well until there are no more flecks of white, then pour in the stock or water. Stir constantly over low heat until the mixture boils. Season with salt and pepper. Strain into a clean saucepan if necessary, reheat and serve.

Bread sauce

Put the onion, thyme, cloves and milk in a saucepan. Bring gently to the boil over low heat. Simmer for 5 minutes. Remove from the heat and set aside for 1 hour. Remove the cloves. Add the breadcrumbs, butter and cream, if using, to the pan. Reheat until nearly boiling. Stir well, then add salt and pepper to taste. Set aside for 10 minutes to thicken, then reheat if necessary before serving.

Cranberry relish

Pick over the cranberries and put them in a saucepan. Add the vinegar, ginger, cinnamon, juniper berries and cloves and simmer until the berries begin to break, adding water if it looks like drying out. Add the sugar and cook for about 20 minutes more. Remove the cloves and cinnamon stick. Check the consistency – it should be like a loose jam. If not, simmer a little longer.

Lemon & herb stuffing

Put the eggs, butter, parsley, thyme, lemon zest and juice in a blender and work to a smooth purée. Pour it over the crumbs and mix well. Season to taste with salt and pepper.

Glazed Ham

A very simple way of feeding a lot of people, this recipe gives a little chilli twist to a classic baked ham. Choose a good-quality sweet chilli sauce, ideally one containing a little ginger, garlic and lime juice as this will add a delicious depth of flavour as well as the gentle chilli warmth.

3–4 sprigs of fresh thyme

2 fresh bay leaves

a sprig of fresh parsley

4.5-kg/10-lb. ham on the bone

1 carrot, roughly chopped

1 onion, roughly chopped

2 celery sticks, roughly chopped

7–8 black peppercorns

3 whole cloves

330-ml/12-oz. can or bottle of stout beer
    (eg Guinness or Mackeson)

3 tablespoons sweet chilli sauce

2 tablespoons pure maple syrup

2 tablespoons Dijon mustard

kitchen twine
stovetop casserole dish with lid

Serves 12–14

Tie the thyme, bay leaves and parsley together with some kitchen twine to make a bouquet garni.

Place the ham in the casserole dish, add the bouquet garni, carrot, onion, celery, peppercorns, cloves and beer. Top up with cold water until the ham is covered. Set over medium heat and bring to the boil. Reduce the heat, partially cover with the lid and gently simmer for about 3 hours. If it starts to look dry, add only boiling water.

At the end of cooking, remove the dish from the heat and set aside for 20–30 minutes to cool with the ham still in the cooking stock.

Preheat the oven to 200°C (400°F) Gas 6.

Remove the ham from the dish and place on a large board. Cut away and discard the skin, leaving an even layer of fat exposed all over the meat. Place the ham in a large roasting pan and, with a sharp knife, score the fat in a diamond pattern, making sure not to cut through to the meat.

Mix the sweet chilli sauce, maple syrup and mustard thoroughly with a balloon whisk. Spread this glaze evenly over the ham, ensuring it is well coated. Roast the ham in the preheated oven for about 30–40 minutes until nicely browned and the glaze has formed a golden crust. Baste the meat with the glaze that runs into the roasting pan during cooking.

Let the ham rest for a few minutes before carving, then serve hot with creamy mustard mashed potato. It can also be served cold.

Roast Beef with all the Trimmings

Only the very best meat should be used for this delicious roast.

3-kg/6-lb. bone-in forerib of beef
   (2–3 bones)

2 tablespoons plain/all-purpose flour

1 tablespoon hot mustard powder

75 g/3 oz. beef dripping, shortening or
   4 tablespoons olive oil

3 onions, quartered

8–10 potatoes, cut into chunks and
   par-boiled

5–6 parsnips, halved lengthways

sea salt and freshly ground black pepper

a large roasting pan

a meat thermometer

Gravy

1 tablespoon fat from the pan

1 onion, thinly sliced

250 ml/1 cup good beef stock

2 teaspoons cornflour/cornstarch, mixed
   with 2 teaspoons cold water

sea salt and freshly ground black pepper

Yorkshire puddings

275 ml/1 cup plus 2 tablespoons milk

2 whole eggs

125 g/1 cup minus 1 tablespoon plain/
   all-purpose flour

½ teaspoon salt

4–6 tablespoons fat from the meat
   roasting pan

a 6-hole Yorkshire pudding/popover tray
or a 12-hole mufffin/cupcake pan

Horseradish sauce

1 large horseradish root

1 tablespoon white wine vinegar

250 ml/1 cup double/heavy cream

sea salt

Serves 6–8

Preheat the oven to 240°C (475°F) Gas 8.

Season the meat, mix the flour and the mustard and pat it onto the beef fat. Put the dripping or oil in the large roasting pan, put the onions in the middle and set the beef, fat side up, on top. Put the potatoes and parsnips around the meat and put the pan in the preheated oven. Cook for 20 minutes then reduce the heat to 190°C (375°F) Gas 5, baste the beef and turn the vegetables in the fat. After 20 minutes baste the beef and turn the potatoes and parsnips again. After a further 30 minutes repeat the basting.

After 20 more minutes have passed, increase the oven temperature to 240°C (475°F) Gas 8 and cook for a further 10 minutes. Insert a meat thermometer into the beef. Take the beef out of the oven now, or when the thermometer registers 60°C (175°F) (or a little below if you like beef very rare). Lift the beef onto a serving dish, add the vegetables and set aside in a warm place. It will go on cooking as it rests.

While the meat is resting make the Gravy, Yorkshire Puddings and Horseradish Sauce (see below). Serve the Yorkshire puddings around the beef or on a separate platter. Put the beef on the table with the horseradish sauce and the gravy in a sauce boat, ready to pour.

Gravy

Put the roasting pan on top of the stove, heat the reserved 1 tablespoon fat, add the onion and cook slowly over low heat until browned, about 30 minutes. Do not let burn. Add the stock and cornflour/cornstarch mixture, then season to taste with salt and pepper. Bring to the boil and simmer for a couple of minutes. Strain if you wish or serve as it is.

Yorkshire puddings

Put the milk, eggs, flour and salt in a bowl and whisk well. Spoon fat from the meat roasting pan between 6-holes (1 tablespoon fat each). Pour in the batter (take care because it will spatter). Cook in a preheated oven at 230°C (450°F) Gas 8 for 15–20 minutes until well risen (cooking time will depend on the size of your puddings). Serve as soon as possible. This recipe will make 6 large puddings or 12 smaller ones.

Horseradish sauce

Scrape the fresh horseradish root clean and grate it finely to give 2 tablespoons. Put in a bowl, add the vinegar and salt and stir well. Add the cream and whisk until it becomes thick and light. Rest it at room temperature for at least 2 hours, but serve the same day.

Pumpkin Roasted with Sage & Onion

Pumpkin is delicious sliced and roasted in olive oil on a bed of sage and sliced onions.
This makes a great accompaniment to roast meats and poultry.

750 g/26 oz. fresh butternut squash or
    pumpkin
6 tablespoons extra virgin olive oil
2 large onions, sliced
12 fresh sage leaves
a pinch of chilli/hot red pepper flakes
1 tablespoon red wine vinegar or
    balsamic vinegar
sea salt and freshly ground black pepper

Serves 4 as a side dish

Preheat the oven to 220°C (425°F) Gas 7.

Scoop the seeds out of the squash and cut away the skin. Cut into long slices or chunks. Pour 4 tablespoons olive oil into a metal or enamel roasting pan and add the onion. Season with salt and pepper and toss well to coat. Scatter the pumpkin over the onion and the sage leaves over the pumpkin. Drizzle with the remaining olive oil and season with chilli/ hot red pepper flakes, salt and pepper. Roast for 25–30 minutes until tender and beginning to brown. Remove from the oven, sprinkle with the vinegar while it is still hot, then serve.

Sprouts & Pancetta

This dish is easy to make and a great way to enjoy this seasonal vegetable.

100 g/4 oz/½ cup cubed pancetta or
    thick-sliced rindless bacon, chopped
750 g/1¾ lbs./7 cups Brussels sprouts,
    trimmed
400 ml/1¾ cups chicken or vegetable
    stock, as preferred
25 g/¼ stick unsalted butter
ground white pepper

Serves 6 as a side dish

Fry the pancetta in a large non-stick frying pan/skillet set over medium heat for 4–5 minutes until crispy and golden, then add the Brussels sprouts and cook for a further 1 minute.

Pour in the stock and simmer for 15-20 mins until the sprouts are tender and the stock has reduced. Melt in the butter, season generously with pepper but there is no need to add salt as the pancetta is already salty.

Bacon Rolls

These little bites are very moreish and a great accompaniment to a roast turkey.

9 rindless bacon slices, preferably
    smoked streaky

3 metal kebab/kabob skewers

Serves 6 (allow 3 rolls per person)

Cut the bacon slices in half crossways to give you 18 slices. Roll the bacon up tightly into rolls and spear them on metal skewers – 6 per skewer.

Roast in a preheated oven at 200°C (400°F) Gas 6 for 5 minutes.

Pumpkin Pie

*If you can't find cans of pumpkin purée in your local shops, you can prepare your own –
see the tip below. Alternatively, butternut squash purée makes an ideal substitute and
gives a brighter colour to the filling.*

1 quantity Basic Shortcrust Pastry (see page 130)

475-g/15-oz. can pumpkin purée or 500 ml/2 cups of homemade (see tip)

100 g/½ cup packed soft light brown sugar

3 eggs

200 ml/¾ cup evaporated milk or double/heavy cream

120 ml/½ cup golden syrup/light corn syrup or light molasses

a good pinch of salt

1 teaspoon ground cinnamon

½ teaspoon mixed/apple pie spice

1 teaspoon pure vanilla extract

2 tablespoons golden or spiced rum (optional)

*20.5-cm/8-inch metal or enamel pie plate
a maple leaf pastry cutter (optional*

Serves 4–6

Preheat the oven to 190°C (375°F) Gas 5.

Roll out the pastry thinly on a lightly floured surface and use it to line the pie plate, trimming off the excess pastry. Either crimp the edge of the pastry or use the pastry trimmings to cut leaves to decorate the edge. Prick the base all over with a fork, then line with baking parchment or kitchen foil and baking beans and bake blind for 12–15 minutes. Remove the foil and beans and return to the oven for a further 5 minutes to dry out the pastry. Leave to cool.

Reduce the oven temperature to 160°C (325°F) Gas 3.

Place all the remaining ingredients in a food processor and process until smooth. Set the cooled pie crust on a baking sheet and pour in the filling. Bake in the preheated oven for about 1 hour or until just set. If the pastry edges are beginning to brown too much before the filling is set, cover the edges with kitchen foil before returning to the oven. Remove from the oven to a wire rack and leave to cool in the pie plate. Serve warm or at room temperature, not chilled.

Tip: If you can't find cans of pumpkin or butternut squash purée, you can prepare your own. Cut 750 g/1½ lbs. of unpeeled pumpkin or squash into large chunks and bake in an oven preheated to 160°C (325°F) Gas 3 for about 1 hour. Alternatively, cook the chunks of pumpkin in the microwave in a covered heatproof bowl. (Boiling it won't work as it will make the pumpkin too wet.) When cooled, scrape the flesh from the skin and purée in a food processor.

Brown Sugar Pavlova with Cinnamon Cream & Pomegranate

This is a perfect winter party piece. In summer, top the meringue with fresh berries.

4 large egg whites

50 g/¼ cup packed light muscovado sugar

175 g/¾ cup (caster) sugar (unrefined is best here)

1 teaspoon cornflour/cornstarch

1 teaspoon white wine vinegar

300 ml/1¼ cups double/heavy or whipping cream

1 tablespoon icing/ confectioners' sugar

1½ teaspoons ground cinnamon

150 g/1 cup pomegranate seeds

baking sheet, lined with baking parchment (don't grease it, or your egg whites will collapse!)

Serves 8

Preheat the oven to 140°C (275°F) Gas 1.

Put the egg whites in a large, scrupulously clean bowl and whisk with an electric whisk (or use an electric mixer) until they form stiff peaks. Add the sugars, a tablespoon at a time, whisking constantly. Add the cornflour/cornstarch and vinegar with the final addition of sugar.

Pile the meringue mixture onto the prepared baking sheet and form into a circle about 23 cm/9 inches in diameter. Make swirls in the meringue with a skewer or the end of a teaspoon. Bake in the preheated oven for 1 hour, then turn the oven off and leave the pavlova in until cold – overnight is ideal.

To finish, whip the cream with the icing/confectioners' sugar and cinnamon to soft peaks. Pile it onto the pavlova and scatter the pomegranate seeds over the top.

Strawberry Tiramisù

This is an adaptation of the popular dessert, given a light summery twist with the addition of fresh strawberries, crunchy amaretti cookies and rum.

5 amaretti cookies

2 large eggs, separated

400 g/4 cups strawberries, hulled, 100 g/1 cup finely chopped and 300 g/3 cups sliced

40 g/3 tablespoons unrefined caster/superfine sugar

¼ teaspoon vanilla extract

4 tablespoons white rum

250 g/9 oz. mascarpone, softened

3 tablespoons whipping cream

100 ml/⅓ cup pressed apple juice

100-g/4 oz. Savoiardi/sponge fingers

a large, deep-sided glass dessert bowl

Serves 6

Put the biscuits in a polythene bag, seal, then bash with a rolling pin until they look like coarse breadcrumbs.

Beat the yolks in a bowl with an electric hand-held mixer or a whisk until pale yellow and fluffy, gradually adding the sugar. Add the vanilla extract and a tablespoon of rum. Tip the mascarpone into a large bowl, beat with a wooden spoon to soften, then gradually add the egg yolk mixture and beat until smooth. In another bowl, whisk the egg whites until they just hold a soft peak. Fold the chopped strawberries into the mascarpone mixture, then carefully fold in the egg whites. Whip the whipping cream then fold that in too, with a third of the crushed biscuits. Mix the remaining rum with the apple juice. Dip some of the savoiardi in the apple-rum mixture and lay across the base of the bowl. Reserving some sliced strawberries for decoration, arrange a layer of strawberries over the biscuits, then cover with a layer of mascarpone cream. Repeat with more layers, finishing with the mascarpone cream. Cover with clingfilm and chill in the fridge for 5 hours.

About 1 hour before serving, sprinkle the remaining biscuits over the top of the tiramisù and decorate with the remaining strawberries. Return it to the fridge until ready to serve.

Honey & Spice Cake

A traditional Italian Christmas treat from Siena, this cake is packed with honey and spices, candied fruits and nuts and chocolatey cocoa. Perfect to serve after dinner in thin wedges with coffee. Buy candied fruits in large pieces and chop them up for this – the ready-chopped peel used for Christmas cakes just won't do, this is a luxury cake! It will keep for a month in an airtight tin.

100 g/½ cup walnut halves

100 g/½ cup whole skinned hazelnuts

100 g/½ cup blanched almonds

100 g/½ cup candied orange peel

100 g/½ cup candied citron peel

50 g/⅓ cup plain/all-purpose white flour

4 tablespoons cocoa powder

½ teaspoon ground coriander or whole fennel seeds

1 teaspoon freshly ground black pepper

½ teaspoon ground nutmeg

¼ teaspoon ground cloves

1 teaspoon ground cinnamon

100 g/½ cup caster/granulated sugar

225 g/1 cup clear honey

25 g/2 tablespoons unsalted butter

3 tablespoons icing/confectioners' sugar, sifted with ¼ teaspoon each ground nutmeg, cinnamon, black pepper and cloves, for dusting

rice paper

vegetable oil, for oiling

20 cm/8-inch springform cake pan, lightly buttered

Makes one 20-cm/8-inch cake

Line the base and sides of the springform pan with rice paper.

Preheat the oven to 180°C (350°F) Gas 4.

Spread the nuts on a baking sheet and bake in the preheated oven for 10–15 minutes until golden brown. Cool slightly, then roughly chop and transfer into a medium bowl. Turn the oven down to 150°C (300°F) Gas 2.

Finely chop the orange and citron peel and stir into the bowl of nuts. Sift in the flour, cocoa and spices.

Put the sugar, honey and butter in a saucepan and heat gently, stirring occasionally until dissolved. Boil until the syrup reaches the 'soft ball' stage 117°C–120°C (242°F–248°F) on a sugar thermometer. Quickly stir in the nut mixture and pour into the prepared pan. Smooth the surface with an oiled potato masher. Work quickly before the mixture sets. Bake in the preheated oven for 35 minutes. The cake will not brown or set at this stage. Remove from the oven and set the pan on a cooling rack to cool until firm. The cake will harden as it cools.

When cold, remove the pan and trim the rice paper. Dust with the spiced icing/confectioners' sugar. Serve in thin slices with coffee.

Mince Pies

These mince pies have pastry on the bottom, and a sort of melting piped shortbread on top of the mincemeat, rather than a pastry lid.

1 quantity Basic Shortcrust Pastry (see page 130)

225 g/2 sticks unsalted butter, soft

50 g/⅓ cup icing/confectioners' sugar, sifted

1 teaspoon pure vanilla extract

225 g/1¾ cups plain/all-purpose flour

250–300 g/9–10½ oz. luxury mincemeat

7.5-cm/3-inch fluted pastry cutter

12-hole bun pan

piping bag fitted with a star nozzle/tip

Makes 12

On a lightly floured surface, roll out the pastry thinly and cut out 12 rounds. Press the rounds into the holes of the pan. Prick the bases and chill or freeze for 15 minutes.

Make the topping. In a large mixing bowl and using an electric hand-whisk, cream the butter with the sugar and vanilla until very pale, soft and light. Gradually work in the flour, a tablespoon at a time, beating well between each addition. Spoon into the piping bag (keep at warm room temperature or it will not pipe). Fill the tartlets with the mincemeat, then pipe a swirl of paste on top of each. Chill in the fridge for 30 minutes.

Preheat the oven to 180°C (350°F) Gas 4.

Bake the pies in the preheated oven for about 20 minutes until a pale golden brown. Let cool in the pan, then transfer to a wire rack and dust with icing/confectioners' sugar to serve. Serve warm or at room temperature.

Iced Star Biscuits

These well-flavoured cookies are simple to make and are ideal decorations. Pick your favourite festive cookie cutter, then once they are baked, have fun icing and finishing.

150 g/1¼ sticks unsalted butter, at room temperature

100 g/½ cup caster/granulated sugar

finely grated zest and freshly squeezed juice of 1 unwaxed lemon

75 g/3 oz. cream cheese

300 g/2¼ cups plain/all-purpose flour

a good pinch of salt

1 teaspoon ground mixed spice

To decorate

glacé icing (see recipe method), or writing icing pens, edible silver balls, ribbons for hanging etc., as desired

star-shaped cookie cutter or other festive shape of your choice

several baking sheets

Makes about 24

Beat the butter with the sugar and zest using a wooden spoon or electric mixer. Beat in 2 teaspoons of the lemon juice and all the cream cheese. Sift in the flour, salt and mixed spice and work in. When thoroughly combined, remove the dough from the bowl, shape into a ball and wrap in clingfilm/plastic wrap. Chill until firm, about 30 minutes.

Preheat the oven to 180°C (350°F) Gas 4.

Remove the dough from the fridge, unwrap and roll out on a lightly floured work surface until 5 mm/¼ inch thick. Dip the cookie cutter in flour and cut out shapes. Re-roll the trimmings, cut out more shapes and arrange slightly apart on the baking sheets. Bake for 12–15 minutes until just turning golden brown at the edges. Remove from the oven, leave to cool for 3 minutes, then transfer to a wire rack until completely cold. Decorate with glacé icing (see below) or use a writing icing pen. Store in an airtight container and eat within 5 days.

Glacé icing is made with icing/confectioners' sugar and water, plus a little colouring if you like. It will dry firm but not as hard as royal icing. Sift 100 g/heaping ¾ cup sugar into a bowl. Stir in water or lemon juice, a teaspoon at a time, to make a thick icing that can be piped. If you want to spread the icing, add a little more water to make a consistency that runs slowly off the back of the spoon when it is held up above the bowl.

Christmas Truffles

This recipe is great for Christmas as the round truffles can be left plain or decorated with scraps of red and green coloured sugar paste (or ready-roll icing) to look like holly berries and leaves. You can also add a splash of brandy or rum to the mixture.

200 g/8 oz. dark/bittersweet chocolate, coarsely chopped
125 g/1 cup chocolate spongecake crumbs
60 g/⅔ cup ground almonds
unsweetened cocoa powder, to dust

foil petits-fours or mini-muffin cases

Makes about 8–10

Melt the chocolate in a heatproof bowl set over a pan of steaming but not boiling water. Do not let the base of the bowl touch the water. Stir occasionally until melted, then remove the bowl from the heat.

Stir in the spongecake crumbs and ground almonds. When thoroughly combined, cover the bowl and chill until firm, about 30 minutes. The mixture can be kept in the fridge, tightly covered, for up to 3 days.

Using a teaspoon of mixture for each truffle, roll the mixture into neat balls with your hands, then drop into a small bowl of cocoa and shake to lightly coat. Set each truffle in a foil case. Chill until firm, then pack into boxes or store in an airtight container. Keep in a cool place or the fridge and and eat within 1 week.

Chocolate & Cream Fudge

A quick and easy recipe with a rich flavour. and since almost everyone loves fudge, an offering of a few squares of this will put a smile on anyone's face.

100 g/3½ oz. dark/bittersweet chocolate, coarsely chopped
55 g/4 tablespoons unsalted butter, diced
2 tablespoons double/heavy or whipping cream
1 teaspoon vanilla extract or dark rum
1 tablespoon golden/light corn syrup
225 g/scant 2 cups icing/confectioners' sugar, sifted

shallow, 18-cm/8-inch square pan, greased

Makes about 20 pieces

Melt the chocolate and butter in a heatproof bowl set over a pan of steaming but not boiling water. Do not let the base of the bowl touch the water. Stir frequently until melted, then remove the bowl from the heat and gently stir in the cream, then the vanilla extract, followed by the golden syrup.

Using a wooden spoon, then your hands, work in the icing sugar 1 tablespoon at a time, to make a thick, smooth fudge. If the mixture starts to stiffen before all the sugar has been incorporated, return the bowl to the heat for a minute or so.

Transfer the mixture to the prepared tin and press in evenly. Chill until firm, then turn out and cut into squares with a large, sharp knife. Keep in the fridge and eat within 10 days.

Drinks

Peach Blossom Spring

This is a slight deviation of the classic Bellini, adding a little extra kick with the vodka and peach liqueur. Perfect for serving on a summer's evening or before a dinner party.

25 ml/1 oz. vodka

25 ml/1 oz. peach purée

2 teaspoons crème de peche

chilled prosecco, to top up

2 dashes peach bitters

a peach slice, to garnish

Serves 1

Add the vodka, peach purée and crème de peche to a cocktail shaker filled with ice and shake to mix.

Strain into a champagne flute and top up with prosecco. Add two dashes of peach bitters and serve garnished with a fresh peach slice.

Kir Royale

A classic cocktail, the Kir Royale is considered the epitome of chic sophistication. A great drink to serve at parties or as an aperitif.

1 dash crème de cassis

chilled champagne, to top up

Serves 1

Add a small dash of crème de cassis to a champagne flute and gently top with champagne. Stir gently and serve.

Champagne Cocktail

This cocktail has truly stood the test of time, being as popular now as when it was sipped by stars of the silver screen in the 1940s. It's a simple and delicious cocktail that epitomizes the elegance and sophistication of that era. Perfect for a special occasion.

1 white sugar cube

2 dashes Angostura bitters

25 ml/1 oz. brandy

chilled dry champagne, to top up

Serves 1

Place the sugar cube in a champagne flute and moisten with Angostura bitters. Add the brandy, stir, then gently pour in the champagne and serve.

Pomegranate Punch

Babicka is a truly unique Czech vodka that is infused with wormwood (the key ingredient of absinthe) and which works surprisingly well with pomegranate.

500 ml/ 2 cups Babicka vodka, or other
    vodka of your choice
750 ml/3 cups pomegranate juice
500 ml/2 cups fresh grapefruit juice
    (about 5 grapefruits)
250 ml/1 cup fresh lime juice (8 limes)
150 ml/$^2/_3$ cup sugar syrup
500 ml/2 cups soda water, to serve
pared grapefruit zest and fresh mint
    sprigs, to garnish

Serves 10

Put the vodka, the pomegranate, grapefruit and lime juices, and the sugar syrup in a large punch bowl or pitcher filled with ice. Top up with soda water, and stir gently to mix.

Serve in ice-filled highball glasses, garnished with a grapefruit zest spiral and sprigs of fresh mint. (See picture right.)

Air Mail

Make sure you stir the honey into the other ingredients before adding ice or it will harden inside the shaker and not mix properly with the other ingredients.

25 ml/1 oz. gold Puerto Rican-style rum
12.5 ml/$^1/_2$ oz. fresh lime juice
5 ml/1 barspoon clear, runny honey
champagne or other sparkling white
    wine, to top up

Serves 1

Add the rum, lime juice and honey to a cocktail shaker and stir until the honey is dissolved. Add ice and shake to mix.

Strain into a champagne flute, top up with champagne, and serve. (See picture on page 188.)

Paloma Punch

Although it may seem a lot of effort, do use freshly squeezed grapefruit juice for this cocktail to achieve that perfect summer freshness.

500 ml/2 cups reposado tequila
100 ml/$^1/_3$ cup agave syrup
1.5 litres/6 cups fresh grapefruit juice
    (about 15 grapefruits)
60 ml/$^1/_4$ cup fresh lime juice (2 limes)
250 ml/1 cup soda water
salt, for the glasses

Serves 10

Put the tequila, agave syrup and grapefuit juice in a large jug/pitcher filled with ice. Squeeze the limes into the jug and drop the husks in too, reserving one for preparing the glasses. Top up with the soda water and stir gently to mix.

To prepare the glasses, pour some salt onto a plate. Rub the rim of the glasses with the spent lime husk. Turn each glass upside down and place it in the salt so that it coats the rim.

Fill the salt-rimmed glasses with ice, top up with punch and serve. (See picture top left on page 194)

Berry Caipiroska

*Fresh berries not only give this refreshing cocktail a sweet fruitiness, but they also make
a delightfully pretty drink to serve as an aperitif before an alfresco lunch.*

2 oz./50 ml vodka

4 lime wedges

2 white sugar cubes

3 fresh berries (strawberries,
 raspberries and blueberries are all
 good), plus extra to garnish

Serves 1

Muddle all the ingredients in a rock glass with a wooden pestle. Top up with crushed ice
and stir gently to mix.

Serve garnished with a few fresh berries skewered onto a toothpick/cocktail stick.
(See picture opposite, top right.)

Kingston Cooler

Do try to track down orgeat, an almond flavored syrup as it adds a unique flavor.

500 ml/2 cups dark Jamaican rum

100 ml/⅓ cup Wray and Nephew
 overproof rum

250 ml/1 cup fresh lime juice (about 8
 Limes)

100 ml/⅓ cup orgeat syrup

500 ml/2 cups passion fruit juice

500 ml/2 cups pineapple juice

seasonal fresh fruit and fresh mint sprigs,
 to garnish

Serves 10

Add all the ingredients to a large pitcher or punch bowl filled with ice and stir gently
to mix.

Serve in ice-filled glasses garnished with seasonal fruit and mint sprigs. (See picture
opposite, bottom left.)

Garrick Gin Punch

If the dryness of a good London gin is your thing then this is your cocktail.

50 ml/2 oz. London dry gin

25 ml/1 oz. fresh lemon juice

12.5 ml/½ oz. maraschino liqueur

a dash of sugar syrup

2 dashes Angostura bitters

lemon zest, to garnish

Serves 1

Add all the ingredients to a cocktail shaker filled with ice and shake together until the
outside of the shaker starts to frost.

Strain into a frosted coupette glass and serve garnished with a thin piece of lemon
zest.(See picture opposite, bottom right.)

Sherry Cobbler

The Sherry Cobbler was one of 'the' cocktails of the 19th century. Delightfully smooth, this cocktail calls for a smattering of fresh berries or lemon zest to garnish.

500 ml/2 cups Amontillado sherry
100 ml/⅓ cup fresh lemon juice (about
    2½ lemons)
100 ml/⅓ cup fresh orange juice (about
    2 oranges)
100 ml/⅓ cup sugar syrup
150 ml/⅔ cup pineapple purée
lemon and orange zest, to garnish

Serves 10

Add all the ingredients to a punch bowl filled with ice and stir gently to mix.

Serve in punch cups or glasses filled with cracked ice and garnish with pieces of lemon or orange zest. (See picture opposite.)

Hot Buttered Rum

Rum may be the perfect ingredient for a summer Caribbean-style cocktail, but it also happily lends itself to winter nights, with the sweetness of the rum combining with the spices and the brown sugar. Try also adding cinnamon or vanilla for added complexity.

3 teaspoons brown sugar
50 ml/2 oz. dark rum
½ teaspoon allspice
1 teaspoon butter
hot water, to top up
a piece of orange zest studded with
    cloves, to garnish

Serves 1

Warm a heat-resistant glass and add the sugar and a little hot water. Stir until the sugar has dissolved and then add the rum, allspice, and butter. Top up with hot water and stir until the butter has melted.

Garnish with a piece of orange zest studded with cloves, and serve. (See picture right).

Baltimore Eggnog

In essence, eggnog is a mixture of cream (or milk), sugar and beaten egg that can have alcohol added to it, with the dusting of spice really adding extra depth.

25 ml/1 oz. Madeira wine
12.5 ml/½ oz. Cognac
12.5 ml/½ oz. Jamaican rum
a pinch of ground cinnamon
1 tablespoon caster/superfine sugar
1 egg
25 ml/1 oz. double/heavy cream
freshly grated nutmeg, to serve

Serves 1

Add all the ingredients to a cocktail shaker and shake vigorously for 15 seconds.

Pour into glasses and grate over a little nutmeg, to serve. (See picture opposite.)

Mulled Wine

Traditionally made with red wine, sugar, and spices, this drink is always served hot. Try not to let your mixture boil when you heat it as this may impair the flavour.

2 x 75 cl bottles red wine
100 ml/⅓ cup brandy
pared zest and juice of 2 clementines
pared zest of 1 lime
pared zest of 1 lemon
200 g/1 cup caster/superfine sugar
1 cinnamon stick
4 cloves
4 pinches of freshly grated nutmeg
1 split vanilla pod/bean
lemon zest and cinnamon sticks,
    to garnish

Serves 10

Add all the ingredients to a large saucepan and set over medium heat. Simmer gently for about 30 minutes, stirring occasionally. Strain to remove the zest and spices and return to the pan to keep warm over low heat. Serve in heatproof glasses garnished with a strip of lemon zest and a cinnamon stick.

Breakfast in bed

Eggs Benedict (see page 25)

*Honey and apricot breakfast muffins
(see page 21)*

*Simple White bread (see page 145), toasted
served with jam or marmalade of your choice*

To drink

*Raspberry, strawberry and orange juice
(see page 17)*

Freshly brewed breakfast tea

Friends for Brunch

Nutty honey granola (see page 18)

English breakfast quiche (see page 29)

*Baked beans with maple syrup and paprika
(see page 30)*

Hash browns (see page 30)

Blueberry pancakes (see page 22)

Coffee granitas (see page 134)

To drink

*Banana, honey and wheatgerm lassi
(see page 17)*

Freshly brewed ground coffee

Italian al fresco lunch

Fennel and pancetta puffs (see page 47)

Little Tuscan pizzas (see page 72)

Basil, mozzarella and orzo salad (see page 58)

*Fresh beans with pecorino and prosciutto
(see page 53)*

Globe artichokes with fennel (see page 58)

Chilled lemon souffles (see page 125)
OR
Strawberry tiramisù (see page 181)

To drink

Peach blossom spring (see page 191)

Garden picnic

*Ham hock, bean and mint salad with a creamy
mustard dressing (see page 61)*

*Pasta, Parmesan and cherry tomato pies
(see page 95)*

Asparagus and salmon frittata (see page 71)

*The New York deli sandwiches
(see page 76)*

Bread rolls (see page 146)

*Cherry marzipan streusel squares
(see page 153)*

Chocolate chip cookies (see page 157)

To drink

Kingston cooler (see page 195)

French bistro supper

Salmon rillettes with Melba toast
(see page 44)

Coq au left-over red wine (see page 107)
OR
Aubergine and tomato gratin (see page 116)

Apple and calvados croissant butter pudding
(see page 126)

To drink
Kir royale (see page 191)

Diner-style dinner

Creamy tomato and bread soup
(see page 36)

Seriously tasty traditional Texas chilli (see
page 108) with Cornbread (see page 146)
OR
Chicken pot pie (see page 96)

Vanilla rice pudding (see page 126)
OR
Deep-dish toffee apple pie (see page 130)

To drink
Ice cold beer

Rootbeer

Middle-eastern style buffet

Roasted red pepper and walnut dip
(see page 40)

Dolmades with green lentils, currants and herbs
(see page 43)

Greek salad with butter beans (see page 53)

Grated carrot, blood orange and walnut salad
(see page 65)

Pepper, bean and halloumi salad (see page 54)

Smoked mackerel and lemon pâté (see page 39)

Lamb kefta tagine (see page 100)
OR
Rack of lamb stuffed with feta and mint
(see page 107)

Olive and herb bread (see page 149)

Brown sugar pavlova with cinnamon cream
and pomegranate (see page 181)
OR
Moroccan orange cake (see page 162)

Slices of peeled orange sprinkled with ground
cinnamon and shopped pistachios

To drink
Pomegranate punch (see page 192)

Mint tea

Superfood table

Spicy masala kale chips (see page 43)

*Creamy cannellini, leek and sorrel soup
(see page 35)*

*Lentil and artichoke salad with salsa verde
(see page 54)*

*Quinoa with new-season beans, peas and
asparagus (see page 57)*

Vegetable and lentil moussaka (see page 116)

Oaty apple and raisin crumble (see page 129)

To drink

*Cashew nut and mango smoothie
(see page 17)*

Romantic dinner for two

*Blinis with smoked salmon and crème fraîche
(see page 48)*

Turkey escalopes (see page 75)
OR
*Halibut with fennel, olives and tomato
(see page 83)*

Crème brulées (see page 122)

Your choice from Cheese for two (see page 137)

To drink

Kir royale (see page 191)

Beachcomber cook-out

Sangria prawns (see page 80)

Chilli salt squid (see page 44)

*Sardines with campari, peach and fennel
(see page 79)*
OR
*Mussels, fennel and chickpeas in pink wine
(see page 80)*

Key lime pie (see page 133)

To drink

*Airmail cocktails
(see page 192)*

Warming midwinter supper

Smoky chorizo and bean soup (see page 35)

Truffled mac n' cheese (see page 99)
OR
*Pecorino, pepper and pig cheek pasta
(see page 71)*

Deep-dish toffee apple pie (see page 130)

To drink

Hot buttered rum (see page 196)
OR
Mulled wine (see page 199)

Asian feast

Sesame prawn toasts (see page 47)

*Soy salmon, wasabi mash and pak choy
(see page 87)
OR
Pork with chilli and Thai sweet basil
(see page 87)*

*Cashew nut and mango smoothies
(see page 17)*

To drink
Garrick Gin Punch (see page 195)

Birthday tea party

Paloma punch (see page 192)

*A selection of homemade finger sandwiches
with fillings of your choice*

Pancetta and fennel puffs (see page 47)

Blueberry lime friands (see page 157)

Passion fruit butterfly cakes (see page 158)

Coffee blondies (see page 154)

*Red velvet layer cake (see page 165)
OR
Victoria sandwich with fresh mint
and strawberries (see page 161)*

To drink
Berry caipiroskas (see page 195)

Holiday Celebration

*Champagne cocktails
(see page 191)*

*Blinis with smoked salmon and crème fraîche
(see page 48)
OR
Smoked salmon brochettes (see page 48)*

*Pork and chicken liver terrine with pistachios
(see page 39)*

*Your choice from Winter seasonal cheeseboard
or a selection (see page 141)*

*Roast turkey with lemon and herb stuffing
(see page 169)
with Turkey Accompaniments
(see page 170)
OR
Roast beef with all the trimmings
(see page 174)*

Roast potatoes (see page 66)

Sprouts and Pancetta (see page 177)

Dessert table

Pumpkin pie (see page 178)

*Brown sugar pavlova with cinnamon cream
and pomegranate (see page 181)*

Mince pies (see page 185)

Iced star biscuits (see page 185)

Christmas truffles (see page 186)

Baltimore egg nog (see page 199)

Turkey Roasting Times Chart

Allow 350 g/12 oz. per person oven-ready turkey or 500 g/18 oz. per person untrussed weight.
Final internal temperature with an instant-read thermometer should be 82°C/179°F.

trussed weight in kg/lb.	approx. thawing time in refrigerator	high temperature 220°C (425°F) Gas 7 time in minutes	basic temperature 170°C (335°F) Gas 3 time in minutes	finishing temperature 220°C (425°F) Gas 7 time in minutes	total cooking time/minutes	resting time in minutes
4 kg/9 lbs.	65 hours	20	140	30	190	30
5 kg/11 lbs.	70 hours	25	165	30	220	30
6 kg/13 lbs.	75 hours	35	200	30	265	40
7 kg/15½ lbs.	75 hours	40	230	30	300	40
8 kg/17½ lbs.	80 hours	45	230	35	310	50
9 kg/20 lbs.	80 hours	50	245	35	330	60
10 kg/22 lbs	80 hours	50	265	35	350	60

Index

Recipe Credits

Ross Dobson
Dolmades with green lentils, currants & herbs
Smoky chorizo & bean soup
Creamy cannellini, leek & sorrel soup
Greek salad with butter beans
Pepper, bean & halloumi salad
Lentil & artichoke salad with salsa verde
Slow-cooked pork belly with soya beans & miso
Bean & pork ragù with tagliatelle
Chickpea & fresh spinach curry
Simple tomato & basil risotto
Vanilla rice pudding
Oaty apple & raisin crumble
Slow-cooked tomatoes with goats' cheese & garlic toasts
Sesame prawn toasts
Salmon rillettes with Melba toast
Chilli salt squid
Roasted red pepper & walnut dip
Pork & chicken liver terrine with pistachios
Coq au left-over red wine
Lamb kefta tagine

Maxine Clark
Chicken Pot Pie
Creamy tomato & bread soup with basil oil
Deep-dish toffee apple pie
Fillet of beef en croûte
Fresh beans with pecorino & proscuitto
Glorious golden fish pie
Honey & spice cake
Key lime pie
Little Tuscan pizzas
Mince pies
Pancetta & fennel puffs
Pasta, Parmesan & cherry tomato pies
Peaches & raspberries in sparkling wine
Pumpkin pie
Pumpkin roasted with sage & onion
Roasted pork loin

Tonia George
Baked beans with maple syrup & paprika
Baked tomatoes stuffed with goats' cheese & herbs
Banana, honey & wheatgerm lassi
Bircher muesli
Blinis with smoked salmon & crème fraîche
Blueberry pancakes
Cashew nut & mango smoothie
Dairy-free coconut pancakes with lime syrup & mango
Eggs benedict
English breakfast quiche
Hash browns
Huevos rancheros
Nutty honey granola
Raspberry, strawberry & orange juice
Steak and fried egg sandwiches

Jordan Bourke
Aubergine & tomato gratin
Aubergine, Puy lentils & sundried tomatoes with mint oil
Cannellini bean, avocado & mint
Chargrilled asparagus
Chicken & chorizo with mashed squash & romesco
Globe artichokes with fennel
Grated carrots, blood orange & walnuts
Halibut with fennel, olives & tomato
Harissa roast chicken with spiced vegetables
Moroccan orange cake
Quinoa with new-season beans, peas & asparagus
Soy salmon, wasabi mash & pak choy

Ben Reed
Air Mail
Baltimore Eggnog
Berry caipiroska
Champagne cocktail
Garrick gin punch
Hot buttered rum
Kingston cooler
Kir royale
Mulled wine
Paloma punch
Peach blossom spring
Pomegranate punch
Sherry cobbler

Tori Finch
Asparagus & salmon frittata
Basil mozzarella & orzo salad
Ham hock, bean & mint salad with a creamy mustard dressing
Rack of lamb stuffed with feta & mint
Salad of truffled French beans
The New York deli sandwich

Tori Haschka
Mussels, fennel & chickpeas in pink wine
Pecorino, pepper & pig cheek pasta
Sangria prawns
Sardines with campari, peach & fennel
Slow-cooked pork ribs
Turkey escalopes

Sonia Stevenson
Bacon rolls
Roast beef with all the trimmings
Roast potatoes
Roast turkey with lemon & herb stuffing
Roasted vegetables
Turkey accompaniments

Sarah Randell
Blueberry lime friands
Brown sugar pavlova with cinnamon cream & pomegranate
Cherry marzipan streusel squares
Victoria sandwich with fresh mint & strawberries

Emmanuel Hadjiandreou
Bread rolls
Cornbread
Olive & herb bread
Simple white bread

Susannah Blake
Coffee blondies
Coffee granita
Passion fruit butterfly cakes
Rosewater cupcakes

Linda Collister
Chocolate and cream fudge
Christmas truffles
Iced star biscuits

Nadia Arumugam
Beef chow mein
Chicken with yellow bean sauce & rainbow peppers
Pork with chilli & Thai sweet basil

Will Torrent
Apple & calvados croissant butter pudding
Chilled lemon soufflés
Crèmes brûlées

Fiona Beckett
Cheese for two
Seasonal cheese plates
Strawberry tiramisù

Dan May
Glazed ham

Seriously tasty traditional Texas chilli

Laura Washburn
Salmon, basil & Parmesan pasta bake
Truffled Mac 'n' Cheese

Chloe Coker & Jane Montgomery
Honey and apricot muffins
Vegetable and lentil moussaka

Jenna Zoe
Chocolate chip coconut cookies
Spicy masala kale chips

Hannah Miles
Rocky road cheesecake

Annie Rigg
Gingerbread men
Red velvet layer cake

Elsa Petersen-Schepelern
Smoked salmon brochettes
Sprouts and pancetta

Fiona Smith
Smoked mackerel and lemon pâté

Sunil Vijayakar
Lamb rogan josh

Dunja Gulin
Chocolate chip cookies

Picture Credits